CAUSAL NECESSITY

BRIAN SKYRMS

CAUSAL

NECESSITY

A PRAGMATIC
INVESTIGATION OF
THE NECESSITY OF LAWS

YALE UNIVERSITY PRESS

NEW HAVEN
AND
LONDON 1980

Set in VIP Melior type. Printed in the United States of
America by LithoCrafters, Inc., Chelsea, Mass.

Published in Great Britain, Europe, Africa, and Asia (except
Japan) by Yale University Press, Ltd., London. Distributed
in Australia and New Zealand by Book & Film Services,
Artarmon, N.S.W., Australia; and in Japan by Harper & Row,
Publishers, Tokyo Office.

Library of Congress Cataloging in Publication Data

Skyrms, Brian.
  Causal necessity.

  Bibliography: p.
  Includes index.
    1. Necessity (Philosophy) 2. Law
(Philosophy) 3. Causation. 4. Pragmatics.
I. Title.
BD417.S56   110   79-22983
ISBN 0-300-02339-1

FOR MY PARENTS

Contents

Preface

This is a book for metaphysicians, epistemologists, and philosophers of language. I use the probability calculus because I need it for the analysis, but I have taken care to make the development accessible to a general philosophical readership. The elementary facts about probability needed for the main discussion of the book are reviewed in a "probability refresher" appendix. Key concepts are illustrated by simple examples. I have tried never to use technical machinery for its own sake and to always choose the simplest way to make the philosophical point. Those discussions that do require a bit of technical detail are contained in three appendixes and in three short starred sections, IC1, IC2, and IIF, which may be omitted without loss of continuity.

I have had the opportunity to try out some of the ideas in this book in seminars at the University of Illinois at Chicago Circle, the University of California at Berkeley, the University of North Carolina at Chapel Hill, and La Trobe University, and in papers read at a number of places: the eastern and western divisions of the American Philosophical Association, the Philosophy of Science Association, the spring 1977 conference at the University of Western Ontario on conditionals and expected utility, the fall 1978 conference at the University of Pittsburgh on conditional expected utility, Stanford University, California State University at Northridge, UCLA, Melbourne University, Adelaide University, the University of North Carolina at Greensboro, the University of Chicago, and Princeton University; I have learned a great deal from these discussions. In particular, for private discussions or correspondence on points at issue in this book, I would like to thank Leslie Tharp, Neal Grossman, David Malament, Frank Jackson, Patrick Suppes, Abner Shimony, Bas van Fraassen, Hugh Mellor, Alan Gibbard, Bill Harper, Bob Stalnaker, Nancy Cartwright, David Lewis, Richard Jeffrey, Bill Cooper, Charles Chihara, and Carl Hempel. I owe special debts to Brian Ellis and to Ernest Adams, from whom I have learned a great deal about probability conditionals. I would also like to thank Jane Isay and Maureen Bushkovitch of the Yale University Press for encouragement and help in seeing the manuscript into print.

Introduction

The metaphysics of nomic necessity cannot be adequately discussed in isolation from the epistemology and pragmatics of laws. I believe that we should look at the way in which generalizations are confirmed *qua* law and applied *qua* law for our understanding of the nature of the necessity of laws, rather than relying on the imagery of a freefloating metaphysics of possible worlds. The leading idea of this book is that the key to understanding nomic necessity in this way is *invariance*. In particular, I develop a certain concept of probabilistic invariance, called *resiliency*, which I apply throughout. Possible worlds imagery, if desired, should be cashed in terms of invariance.

Certain patterns of phenomena recur throughout the world. It is economical for a thinking animal to form habits of thought connecting various features of a pattern. The habits corresponding to invariant patterns are refined into laws of nature, the residue of the phenomena being regarded as de facto conditions. The lawgiver who loves symmetry and invariance is man, and his affections are founded in biological economics. The distinction between belief in a statement *qua* law and belief in a statement *qua* matter of fact is, then, to be found in the domain of invariance of that belief. Confirmation *qua* law should carry not only the requirement that the evidence warrant high probability, but also that it warrant *invariantly* high probability.

A concept of degree of invariance, the concept of resiliency, is developed in chapter IA and applied to the problem of physical propensities and the nature of statistical laws. In chapter IB the confirmation of universal laws is discussed from this perspective, and it is shown how various well-known puzzles are thereby solved. In part II it is shown how this theory of the confirmation of laws illuminates the connection between laws and conditionals (both indicative and subjunctive), causal relations, scientific explanation, and knowledge (as opposed to mere true belief).

This brief book cannot contain an exhaustive study of even one small area of the epistemology or the pragmatics of laws. I have tried, however, to pack a lot of ideas into a small space—perhaps sometimes to the detriment of the exposition. I hope that the reader will, at least, not be bored, and that s(he) will find here some food for thought.

LAWS

The world is very complicated and it is clearly impossible for the human mind to understand it completely. Man has therefore devised an artifice which permits the complicated nature of the world to be blamed on something which is called accidental and thus permits him to abstract a domain in which simple laws can be found. The complications are called initial conditions; the domain of regularities, laws of nature.

Eugene P. Wigner
"Invariance in Physical Theory"

We must, in short, follow the Baconian Rule for varying the circumstances. This is, indeed, only the first rule of physical inquiry and not, as some have thought, the sole rule; but it is the foundation of all the rest.

J. S. Mill
A System of Logic

No one supposes that a good induction can be arrived at merely by counting cases. The business of strengthening the argument chiefly consists in determining whether the alleged association is stable, when the accompanying conditions are varied.

John Maynard Keynes
A Treatise on Probability

IA Propensities and Statistical Laws

IA1. PROPENSITIES AND STATISTICAL LAWS

By *propensities* I mean the kind of probabilities that figure in laws of nature. Others have used the term to mean something different or something more, or have held that that role implies things that I am not willing to grant it implies. This does not mean that I believe propensities *must* be embedded in laws of nature, but only that propensities are the *sorts* of probabilities that are so embedded.

Let us focus on simple probabilistic laws of the form: "If a physical system is in state F, then the probability that it has property P is a."[1] A typical probabilistic law is, of course, more complicated; but it is typically applied by deriving a statement of the foregoing form. These laws may be generated by statistical treatment of an underlying deterministic process, as in statistical mechanics, or may be, to the best of our knowledge, basic, as in quantum mechanics. Propensities arising from the first sort of law, for example, the propensity of a Brownian particle to migrate a certain distance in a certain time, are not essentially different from propensities generated by homely gambling devices. I will feel free to join the tradition of using coin flips, rolls of a die, or spins of a wheel as stock examples of propensities.

If we have a probabilistic law of the form given, then a physical system with property F at a certain time is said to have at that time a *propensity* to exhibit P with probability a. F may be called the *foundation* for the propensity. Propensities attach, in the first analysis, to *single cases:*[2]

1. Or, perhaps, "The probability that it has P given that it is in state F is a."
2. A point made forcefully by R. Giere in "Objective Single-Case Probabilities and the Foundations of Statistics," in P. Suppes et al., eds., *Logic, Methodology and Philosophy of Science IV* (Amsterdam: North Holland, 1973), pp. 468–83. See also, B. De Finetti, *Theory of Probability* (New York: Wiley, 1975) and *Probability, Induction and Statistics* (New

the probability that a given flip will come up heads, that a
certain incident of exposure to a disease vector will produce infection, and so forth. We might want to say that
propensities attach to individual events rather than event
types, but I prefer to interpret propensities as attaching to
propositions (or sentences), rather than to propositional
functions. Given the current philosophical debate over the
correct way of individuating events, this at least has the
advantage of being a more specific proposal. It is, perhaps,
also a more correct proposal in that it makes explicit pro-
vision for the intensionality of probabilistic contexts. The
next toss tnat comes up heads may in fact be identical to
toss 36, but the probability that toss 36 comes up heads
may be quite different from the probability that the next
toss that comes up heads comes up heads. Such blatant
examples of intensionality are usually avoided by statisticians by refraining from the use of information-packed
definite descriptions as the designators of choice. Still, intensionality is present in statistical practice in a subtler
way, when the order of the numbers used as names may or
may not be thought of as conveying information as to the
temporal order of the trials.

When we infer a statement of propensity from a statistical law, the inference appears to be a type of universal
specification. From:

>   Every trial (system at a time), x, such that Fx has
> $pr(Px) = a$

and

>   Trial c has F

we infer:

> $pr(P$ on trial $c) = a$

by universal specification and detachment.[3] Universal
specification into intensional contexts has its pitfalls,
which are well enough known to philosophers of language and practitioners of modal logic. In probability, the
problem for frequentists who wish to give the primary in-

York: Wiley, 1974), and H. Mellor, *The Matter of Chance* (Cambridge:
Cambridge University Press, 1971).

    3. P. Railton makes this point in connection with the logic of statis-
tical explanation in "A Deductive-Nomological Model of Probabilistic
Explanation," *Philosophy of Science* 45 (1978):206–26.

terpretation of probability to propositional functions, as in the law, has become infamous as the *problem of the single case.* One who takes the notion of probabilities of propositions as basic, as I do here, must tackle the same problem from the other end: how is the intensionality problem to be handled so that statistical laws and their instances mesh properly?

IA2. EXCHANGEABILITY AND UNIVERSAL SPECIFICATION

The philosophers penchant for complete generality may sometimes be counterproductive; it may divert attention from special cases in which a problem has a straightforward solution. I want here to focus on a probabilistic special case which illuminates the problem of universal specification, and which, in the final analysis, may prove to be less special than it at first appears.

Suppose that we have an experimental arrangement which is about to produce a series of experimental results. We will name the trials of the experiment with numerals in such a way that the numerical order corresponds to the temporal order of the trials. The probabilities that we attach to this experimental arrangement may be such that this order is not important. That is, the probability of an outcome, H, on trial 1 may be equal to the probability of that outcome on any later trial, the probability of H on 1 and T on 36 may be equal to the probability of T on 1 and H on 36, and generally the probability of any sentence describing outcomes may be invariant under permutations of outcomes. In such a case the trials are said to be, in De Finetti's terminology, *exchangeable.*[4] (We should be careful to bear in mind, however, that exchangeability attaches to a probability over a field of *propositions* about outcomes on trials.)

Sequences of exchangeable trials are important for several reasons. The one I want to stress here is that in such a sequence we have a well-defined sense of the probability of a *property* (an outcome type, e.g., heads) which

4. R. Carnap and L. J. Savage would say that such a measure is *symmetric.*

is derivative from probabilities of *propositions* (single cases, outcome type on a trial, heads on 1). The probability of a property is just the probability that that property is exhibited on a trial—*any trial,* for by the hypothesis of exchangeability that probability is the same for any trial.

If the probability in a statistical law is thought of as referring to such an exchangeable sequence, then the universal specification which gives us single-case propensities holds no mystery.[5] The problem of intensionality is solved by choosing standard names for trials, such that exchangeability ensues. Universal specification (and existential generalization) are tacitly restricted to these standard names. We still cannot universally specify to "the next trial that comes up heads" or "the next time interval in which the atom decays." Nor can we specify to trials whose outcomes we *know*, if that knowledge is reflected in our probability distribution, for then we no longer have exchangeability. If we know that the atom *did* decay on trial 1, and therefore assign probability one to "decay on trial 1," then we must exclude trial 1 from the domain to which we can universally specify our statistical law and still get correct results. (Otherwise we could falsify all statistical laws just by *watching what happens!*)

These consequences of exchangeability are so pleasant that it is a shame that exchangeability is a special case. But it is not as special as it first seems. The way in which I motivated exchangeability—by first correlating the temporal order of the trials with a natural order of the names of the trials and then insisting that that order is irrelevant to the probabilities—must strike the reader as perverse.[6]

5. I find this insight, though not quite in these terms, already in B. De Finetti, "Foresight, Its Logical Laws, Its Subjective Sources," in H. Kyberg and H. Smokler, eds., *Studies in Subjective Probability* (New York: Wiley, 1964). Compare the remarks of W. Salmon and P. Railton on maximal specificity in, respectively, *Statistical Explanation and Statistical Relevance* (Pittsburgh: University of Pittsburgh Press, 1971) and "A Deductive-Nomological Model of Probabilistic Explanation," *Philosophy of Science* 45 (1978):206–26, and those of H. Reichenbach on "the narrowest reference class for which we have reliable statistics" in *The Theory of Probability* (Berkeley and Los Angeles: University of California Press, 1949).

6. Thus making explicit what is customarily assumed in the theory of stochastic processes.

Why make the correlation in the first place? Suppose the names are assigned at random to the unexamined trials, so that the names themselves carry no information as to order. Then it would be most natural for our epistemic probabilities to make these unexamined trials exchangeable, even if temporal order is important.

But would such a convention of "blind" names not preclude an adequate treatment of important types of stochastic processes where order does make a difference? It is not so bad as one might think. Information that has been washed out of the names can be carried by new predicates. Consider the case of a Markov process where the probability of an outcome on a trial depends on the outcome of the previous trial. We can represent this in a new language which contains not only the old outcome predicates H, T, but also the new predicates *preceded by an* H, *preceded by a* T.

Since the problem of universal specification (the *de dicto –de re* problem, the problem of the single case) ceases to be a problem when we have exchangeability, we might think of the foregoing procedure as supplying a *canonical form* for expressing probabilities when we want to think about these issues. (For other purposes, of course, the usual method of representation may be more convenient.)

Another kind of problem of the single case would arise if we had two well-confirmed laws: "If Fx then $Pr(Gx) = a$" and "If $F'x$ then $Pr(Gx) = b$" where $a \neq b$ and F is compatible with F'. Then for a physical system, s, such that Fs and $F's$ we are faced with the question of which value to take as $Pr(Gx)$. This version of the problem of the single case calls for consideration of a more general kind of invariance, to which we will proceed in the next section.

IA3. RESILIENCY, NECESSITY, AND RANDOMNESS

This is what writers mean when they say that the notion of cause involves the notion of necessity. If there be any meaning which confessedly belongs to the term necessity, it is unconditionalness. *That which is necessary, that which* must be, *means that which will be, whatever supposition we make with regard to other things. . . . We*

*may define, therefore, the cause of a phenomenon, to be
the antecedent, or concurrence of antecedents, on which
it is invariably and* unconditionally *consequent.*

J. S. Mill
A System of Logic

---

*If the term randomness is to include further requirements,
they can be stated by the use of selections of physical
reference—selections not defined by mathematical rules,
but by reference to physical (or psychological) occur-
rences. For practical statistics it is as important to know
which physical selections belong to the domain of invariance as it is to know which mathematical selections are
contained in this domain. If a sequence possesses randomness of the von Mises—Church type, there may still be
physical selections that lead to a deviating frequency.*

Hans Reichenbach
The Theory of Probability

Exchangeability is one species of *invariance* of probabilities, invariance under permutations of names. I want
here to consider invariance more generally.[7] Suppose that
I have a set of propositions, p_1, p_2 . . . To say that q is
statistically independent of each of these, is to say that q
is *invariant under conditionalization* on these; that is, the
unconditional probability of q is equal to the conditional
probability of q given p_i for each p_i in the set. If we view
conditionalization as an important way in which probabilities can evolve in time, invariance under conditionalization is a kind of *stability* property for probabilities.[8]

7. Exchangeability can be thought of as a special case as follows: if
we have exchangeability, we can introduce a new name, a, such that for
any outcome type, O, Pr (O on a) is invariant under conditionalization on
the propositions: a = trial 1, a = trial 2, etc.

8. The importance of stability under conditionalization was already
recognized and studied by Wilhelm Lexis and his followers in the 1870s.
See Lexis, "Die Theorie der Stabilität statistischer Reihen," in
Abhandlungen zur Theorie der Bevölkerungs- und Moral Statistik (Jena,

Instead of considering only absolute independence, I wish to also consider cases of approximate independence. I can get a measure of approximate independence of q from $p_1, p_2 \ldots$ by seeing how much $Pr(q)$ wiggles under conditionalization on the p_is. The amplitude of the wiggle[9] is: maximum $|Pr(q) - Pr(q \text{ given } p_i)|$. It will be convenient to take our measure of approximate invariance under conditionalization over the p_is, as *one minus the amplitude of the wiggle*:

Degree of invariance of $Pr(q) = 1 - Max_i|Pr(q) - Pr(q \text{ given } p_i)|$ over the p_is

In this way, the more invariant a probability is, the higher the measure of approximate invariance, with a measure of 1 corresponding to absolute invariance, or statistical independence.

Given a finite set of sentences, $p_1 \ldots p_n$, we might be interested not only in the degree of invariance of $Pr(q)$ under conditionalization on these sentences, but also in the degree of invariance under conditionalization on any (consistent) truth-functional combination of these sentences. (In the most general case, the p_is may not be logically independent of q. In this case, we avoid trivializing the question by asking for the degree of invariance of $Pr(q)$ under conditionalization on truth-functional combinations of the p_is that are logically consistent with both q and $\sim q$.) This quantity I call the *resiliency* of $Pr(q)$ over the p_is. To generalize a little bit more, if α is a number, I can talk of the *resiliency of* $Pr(q)$ *being* α as 1 minus the amplitude of the wiggle about α, whether or not the probability of q actually is exactly α or not. Thus, most generally:

Resiliency of $Pr(q)$s being $\alpha = 1 - Max_i|\alpha - Pr_j(q)|$ over $p_1 \ldots p_n$

(where the Pr_js are gotten by conditionalizing on

1903) and von Bortkiewicz, *Homogeneität und Stabilität in der Statistik* (Uppsala, 1918). The ideas of the school of Lexis reached English-speaking statisticians via F. Y. Edgeworth, and again later via J. M. Keynes and L. von Mises.

9. Of course, measures of dispersion other than this could be used to give slightly different notions of approximate independence. My reasons for focusing on this particular measure will emerge in chapter IB.

some truth-functional compound of the p_is which
is logically consistent with both q and its negation)

Since in an exchangeable sequence of trials we have an
unambiguous sense in which probabilities attach to properties, we also have an unambiguous sense in which we
can talk about the *resiliency of the probability of a property being present over some list of other properties or experimental factors*. In this way, the idea of invariance of
probabilities of experimental results under variation of
combinations of experimental factors is represented by
high resiliency. I will feel free to talk this way with the
understanding that, when I do so, an exchangeable sequence of trials and the construction of property probabilities out of proposition probabilities are presumed.

One can define resiliency for conditional probabilities
in an analogous way as one minus the amplitude of the
wiggle:

Resiliency of $Pr(q$ given $r)$ being $\alpha = 1 - Max_i|\alpha - Pr_j(q$ given $r)|$ over $p_1 \ldots p_n$
(Where the Pr_js are gotten by conditionalizing on
some truth-functional compound of the p_i that is
logically consistent with $p \& q$ and with $p \& \sim q$)

Here is another way of looking at resiliency of a conditional probability. Let us define the *resiliency* $Pr(q)$ *being
α conditional on* r, as the resiliency of $Pr(q)$ being α in the
probability distribution gotten by conditionalizing on r.
This conditional resiliency is then equal to Resiliency of
$Pr(q$ given $r)$ being α. *Conditional resiliency equals resiliency of the corresponding conditional probability.*[10]

High resiliency can be thought of as a statistical notion
of *necessity*. As Mill remarks: "If there be any meaning
which confessedly belongs to the term necessity, it is *unconditionalness*. That which is necessary, that which
must be, means that which will be whatever supposition
we make with regard to other things."[11] If the resiliency of

10. Provided that the corresponding conditional probability is well
defined.
11. J. S. Mill, *A System of Logic*, 8th ed., bk. 3, ch. 5, sec. 6 (New
York: Harper, 1874).

$Pr(q)$ being α is near (or equal to) 1, then $Pr(q)$ is near (or equal to) α conditional on every supposition consistent with q, $\sim q$ that we can frame in terms of the sentences over which the resiliency is evaluated. The modal logician might like to think of these suppositions as specifications of classes of possible worlds, or alternatively as precise specifications of the probability distributions "accessible from" the current one by conditionalization on them. If the resiliency of $Pr(q) = \alpha$ is one, then $Pr(q)$ *is* α and would still be α over a whole range of possible modifications of our probability distribution by conditionalization.

> Necessity = Unconditionality = Invariance = Independence.[12]

There is yet another perspective from which to view this concept and that is as a generalized version of *randomness*. According to von Mises, an infinite sequence (e.g., tosses of a coin) is to be random with respect to its outcomes (e.g., heads, tails) just in case the relative frequency of the outcomes remains unchanged in all subsequences gotten from the original sequence by "place selection." Von Mises's explanation of the intuitive idea behind "place selection" has, for a frequentist, a curiously epistemological flavor:

> By place selection, we mean the selection of a partial sequence in such a way that we decide whether an element should or should not be included without making use of the attribute of the element. (*Probability Statistics and Truth*, p. 25)

Von Mises tried to make this idea precise by identifying place selection as selection by a characteristic function: a function which takes as arguments initial segments of the sequence and as values zero (signifying "next member not selected for the subsequence") and one (signifying "next member selected"). Of course, with the set-theoretic sense of function this will not do, for there are enough functions around to upset the claim to randomness of *all* sequences

---

12. Note that here we mean statistical independence in general, not just independence of *trials*.

(excepting a few degenerate ones). Take an infinite sequence of heads and tails. Consider the function which maps an initial segment of the sequence on to the value one just in case the next element is heads. There is such a function in the set-theoretic sense, although the way I have specified it may seem a little underhanded. And provided there was an infinite number of heads in the original sequence, it will select out an infinite subsequence consisting entirely of heads. Likewise with tails. The problem is that the epistemic clause of the informal definition "without making use of the attribute of the element" has no restrictive role to play in this account.

What one can have in a nonvacuous way is a notion of randomness relativized to a certain class of place-selection functions. Wald showed that relative to an arbitrary denumerable class of place-selection functions, there is a continuum of random sequences. Church suggests taking a particularly natural set of place-selection functions—the recursive ones.

It should be clear that these ideas of randomness are also closely connected with resiliency. For every place-selection function there is a corresponding property which selects out the subsequence (e.g., the property of following the initial segment TTT, or the initial segment $TTTH$, or the initial segment $TTTHHT$, and so forth. Resiliency of one over the instantiations of this class of properties will guarantee randomness relative to the associated class of place-selection functions (and will coincide with it provided that the class of properties has the appropriate Boolean closure property).

We might view high resiliency as a natural generalization of von Mises's original definition of randomness. In fact, Reichenbach objects that the direction suggested by Church construes the invariance too narrowly for the intended physical applications: "If a sequence possesses randomness of the von Mises–Church type there may still be *physical* selections that lead to a deviating frequency."[13] That is, some physical property (e.g., tempera-

13. H. Reichenbach, *Theory of Probability* (Berkeley and Los Angeles: University of California Press, 1949), p. 150.

ture below −200 degrees C.) might select out a subsequence, or subensemble, which changed the frequency
(and thus called for qualification of the associated physical law or propensity statement). Let us call Reichenbach's idea of invariance under selection of subsequence
by an arbitrary physical property *physical randomness.*

The *absolute* concept of physical randomness is
clearly in as much trouble as von Mises' original definition. Just what physical properties *exist* is a tricky physical question. If we take the extensional route of identifying physical properties with classes of physical events, we
will have a bit of difficulty finding physically random sequences. But even without indulging in such dubious
metaphysical identifications, we can see that the concept
of absolute physical randomness is suspect. Consider the
paradigm case of radioactive decay. We can select subsequences with different relative frequencies simply by
referring to the readings of detectors placed in the vicin-
ity. There seems to me to be no reason to believe that we
could not always, by referring to the results of physical
measurements, select out subsequences with variant relative frequencies. The only sort of physical randomness
that makes sense, then, is randomness relative to a given
set of physical properties. (There is no *absolute* physical
randomness. There is no *absolute* resiliency.)

Von Mises and Reichenbach are both working within a
framework in which probability is interpreted as limiting
relative frequency. They differ in that von Mises takes
randomness as essential to the concept of probability,
whereas Reichenbach, realizing the relative nature of randomness, treats it as an important family of special cases
of probability. The concept is not, however, essentially
tied to frequentism; it may be applied to any probability
distribution, whatever its interpretation. We can think of
randomness relative to a set of sentences as invariance
under conditionalization on them. In the case of exchangeable sequences, we then can talk with Reichenbach
about invariance over a set of physical properties or factors. Resiliency is, in this generalized sense, a measure of
degree of randomness.

Resiliency of probability values in its many guises is

such an important and central concern that *it is not surprising that standard scientific methodology aims at achieving resilient probability values*. The principle of the variety of instances has been recognized as a canon of scientific methodology by every serious student of induction since Bacon. Carnap writes: "One of the principles of the methodology of induction says that in testing a law we should vary as much as possible the conditions that are not specified in the law. This principle is generally recognized, and scientists followed it long before it was formulated explicitly."[14] Mill says: "We must, in short, follow the Baconian Rule of *varying the circumstances*. This is, indeed, only the first rule of physical inquiry, and not, as some have thought. the sole rule; but it is the foundation of all the rest";[15] and he heeds his own injunction in his analysis of the "four methods of experimental inquiry." Keynes opens his discussion of Lexis as follows: "No one supposes that a good induction can be arrived at merely by counting cases. The business of strengthening the argument chiefly consists of determining when the alleged association is *stable*, when the accompanying conditions are varied."[16]

Attempts to explain the prominence of this principle in Keynes and Carnap appear somewhat strained. The problem is, I think, that scientific laws are here thought of as universal laws; that universal laws are thought of as universally quantified material conditionals; and that the business of science is thought of as achieving high epistemic probability for those universal generalizations thought of as scientific laws. On this view, something can be said for the principle of variety of instances, but hardly enough. We attain a fresher perspective, I think, if we first focus on the case of statistical laws and only later try to fit in the case of universal laws.

It is certainly to our advantage if our statistical laws give us probabilities that are stable, and if propensities are

14. *Logical Foundations of Probability*, 2d ed. (Chicago: University of Chicago Press, 1962), p. 230.

15. J. S. Mill, *System of Logic*, bk. 3, ch. 7, sec. 1.

16. J. M. Keynes, *A Treatise on Probability* (London: Macmillan, 1952), p. 393.

stable probabilities; and I shall argue in the second part of this book that much of the pragmatics of laws assumes such stability. The point here is that the Baconian rule of varying the circumstances has a straightforward interpretation as a rule aimed at guaranteeing that such stability is attained. I am suggesting, then, that for a statistical law, "If a physical system is in state F, then the probability that it has P is a," to be well confirmed qua law, the resiliency of $Pr(Px)$[17] being a, conditional on F, must be high. I think that it is a more faithful representation of scientific practice to bring resiliency in by the front door as a desideratum for the probabilities in laws, rather that bringing the requirement of the variety of instances in by the back door solely on the excuse that it may augment the epistemic probability of universally quantified material conditionals.

A propensity, then, will be a highly resilient probability, and a statistical law will tell us that a physical system which fulfills the requisite condition has the corresponding propensity.

Let us call the list of propositions (or factors) over which a probability ascription is highly resilient the *scope* of the resiliency. The term is vague and is introduced only for a brief, but I hope suggestive, discussion of several examples. The first is from A. J. Ayer's classic paper "What Is a Law of Nature?" where he suggests a kind of resiliency requirement for lawlikeness:

> Thus, I believe that all the cigarettes in this case were made of Virginia tobacco, but this belief would be destroyed if I were informed that I have absentmindedly just filled my case from a box in which I keep only Turkish cigarettes.[18]

The second is from Max Planck's survey of physical theory:

17. X being a blind name in an exchangeable sequence of trials as previously discussed.

18. A. J. Ayer, "What Is a Law of Nature?" *Revue internationale de philosophie* 10.2 (1956):144–65. Reprinted in Ayer, *The Concept of a Person* (New York: St. Martin's, 1963) and in J. Beauchamp, ed., *Philosophical Problems of Causation* (Encino, Cal.: Dickenson, 1974).

How is it that a definite Uranium atom, after having
remained completely unaltered and passive for untold
millions of years, suddenly, in an immeasurably short
space of time, without any determinable cause,
explodes with a violence, compared with which our
most powerful explosives are like toy pistols? It sends
off fragments of itself with velocities of thousands of
kilometers per second, and at the same time emits
electromagnetic rays of greater intensity than the hard-
est Röntgen rays, while another atom in its neighbor-
hood, and to all appearances exactly similar, remains
in a passive state for still more millions of years until it
finally meets the same fate. In fact, all attempts to af-
fect the course of radio-active phenomena by external
means, such as raising or lowering of temperature,
have ended in complete failure.[19]

As an example having somewhat more scope than Ayer's,
but not much more, we might take the probabilities that
actuaries calculate for insurance companies. As an example having somewhat less scope than the ultimate
quantum-mechanical case, we might take the statistical
laws of Brownian motion. Somewhere in the middle we
may find the classical gambling devices, dice shaken and
rolled vigorously from a cup against a wall studded with
little rubber cones, and so forth. Some people might prefer
to reserve the term *propensity* for the nicest cases, where
the scope is as great as it is in quantum mechanics, but I
prefer to be more easygoing. Some might argue that any
laws whose scope falls short of quantum-mechanical laws
(and all others do) are not laws at all. But I prefer to be able
to talk of laws down to the level of statistical mechanics
and Brownian motion.[20] Things are not so well behaved
there. Probabilities are not invariant over microdescrip-
tions, but that's life.

I believe that the place to look for the modal component in propensities and statistical laws is just here: in the

19. *A Survey of Physical Theory* (New York: Dover, 1960).
20. Ergodic theory can be viewed as an investigation of the scope of
resiliency in statistical mechanics.

resiliency (physical randomness, stability, invariance under conditionalization, etc.) of the probabilities involved. Things are not as clean-cut as one might hope. We find no absolute resiliency in physics, nice as it would be if we did. And philosophers have no business trying to lay down, a priori, standards for the scope of resiliency appropriate to physical theories. Standards for resiliency evolve along with physical theory in a big virtuous circle, and in our dealings with nature we take what we can get.

IA4. EPISTEMIC PROBABILITIES, OBJECTIVE PROBABILITIES AND PROPENSITIES

I, therefore, feel warranted in affirming that Laplace has overlooked, in this general theoretical statement, a necessary part of the foundation of the doctrine of chances.

---

§ 2. To be able to pronounce two events equally probable, it is not enough that we should know that one or the other must happen, and should have no ground for conjecturing which. Experience must have shown that the two events are of equally frequent occurrence. Why, in tossing up a halfpenny, do we reckon it equally probable that we shall throw cross or pile? Because experience has shown that in any great number of throws, cross and pile are thrown about equally often; and that the more throws we make, the more nearly the equality is perfect. . . .

It would indeed require strong evidence to persuade any rational person that by a system of operations upon numbers, our ignorance can be coined into science.

J. S. Mill
A System of Logic (1st ed., 1843), ch. 18, secs. 1,2

This view of the subject was taken in the first edition of the present work; but I have since become convinced that the theory of chances, as conceived by Laplace and by mathematicians generally, has not the fundamental fallacy which I had ascribed to it.

We must remember that the probability of an event is not a quality of the event itself, but a mere name for the degree of ground which we, or some one else, have for expecting it. The probability of an event to one person is a different thing from the probability of the same event to another, or to the same person after he has acquired additional evidence. The probability to me, that an individual of whom I know nothing but his name will die within the year, is totally altered by my being told the next minute that he is in the last stage of a consumption. Yet this makes no difference in the event itself, nor in any of the causes on which it depends. Every event is in itself certain, not probable; if we knew all, we should either know positively that it will happen, or positively that it will not. But its probability to us means the degree of expectation of its occurrence, which we are warranted in entertaining by our present evidence.

J. S. Mill
A System of Logic (8th ed., 1874), ch. 18, sec. 1.

By *epistemic probability*, I mean degree of rational belief.[21] I assume that the constraints of rationality assure enough coherence to permit a probability representation. The constraints of rationality no doubt require a great deal more; to say what more is the chief business of epistemology. I will not attempt to say anything on that subject here.

There are situations in which we wish to distinguish "objective" probabilities, and in particular *propensities*, from epistemic probabilities. Suppose that we know that a coin is either biased two to one in favor of heads or two to one in favor of tails (I abbreviate the first proposition as *BH*, the second as *BT*). We want to say that if the first proposition is true, the propensity of getting heads is 2/3; if

21. I prefer to avoid the term *subjective* since it suggests that the qualification of rationality has been omitted.

the second proposition is true, then the propensity of getting heads is 1/3. But we simply may not be in a position to know which way the coin is biased, so we may be uncertain as to which propensities obtain. We thus have two propensity distributions, pr_{BH} and pr_{BT}. How should they figure in the epistemic probability that the next toss will come up heads?

If we accept the most plausible principle:

Principle M: The epistemic probability of H, conditional on the proposition that the objective probability of H is a, is a

then it follows that we should average the propensity distributions to get our epistemic distribution, using as weights for the average the epistemic probabilities attaching to the respective propensity distributions.[22] Writing epistemic probability in capitals, we have in our example:

$$PR(H) = PR(BH)\, pr_{BH}(H) + PR(BT)\, pr_{BT}(H)$$

Here we get epistemic probabilities from uncertain objective probabilities by taking a weighted average (a mixture), with the weights being the epistemic probabilities attaching to that distribution. Another way of saying this is to say that epistemic probability is the epistemic expectation of objective probability.[23]

Suppose that relative to a certain decomposition of our epistemic probabilities into objective probabilities (e.g., pr_{BH} and pr_{BH}) a bit of information or reflection leads us to change our epistemic probabilities solely by changing the proportions in which the objective probabilities are mixed. Let the new proportions be α for pr_{BH} and $(1 - \alpha)$ for pr_{BT}. Then the new epistemic probability of any statement q, $PR_{new}(q)$, can be written in terms of the old epistemic probabilities as:

$$PR_{new}(q) = PR_{old}(q\ given\ BH) + (1 - \alpha)\, PR_{old}(q\ given\ BT)$$

This sort of change is called probability kinematics[24] be-

22. See appendix 2 for a fuller discussion of principle M.

23. See appendixes 1 and 2.

24. By R. Jeffrey, in The Logic of Decision (New York: Macmillan, 1965). The status of probability kinematics is discussed in greater detail in appendix 2.

cause of the rigidity of the probabilities conditional on the characteristic propositions of the objective distributions.

Having mixed the objective probabilities to get the epistemic distribution, is there any way of reversing the process, of "unmixing" the epistemic distribution to get the objective distributions? Yes. We can "unmix" by conditionalizing on those characteristic propositions of the objective distributions whose epistemic probability we used to weight the original mixture. The objective probabilities are equal to conditional epistemic probabilities, thus:

$$pr_{BH}(q) = PR(q \text{ given } BH)^{25}$$
$$pr_{BT}(q) = PR(q \text{ given } BT)$$

Objective probabilities are gotten from epistemic probabilities by conditionalizing out.[26]

Given an epistemic probability distribution and a way of dividing up the possibilities into mutually exclusive and exhaustive classes (*BH* and *BT* in our example), we can always decompose into "objective" distributions by conditionalizing out in the manner indicated. And relative to such a partition of possibilities we can think of the "true objective probability" as the probability in the objective distribution whose characteristic proposition (e.g., *BH*) is true. But given that we can decompose into "objective" probability distributions in more than one way, we may be tempted to ask: "What is the *right* way to decompose to get the *right* objective probabilities?"

I think that the question is a mistake. There is no unique correct way to decompose. The most specific way to decompose will, after all, give us all probability values of either zero or one. Mill, I think, takes the proper attitude toward this matter in discussing the partition of factors presupposed by his methods of experimental inquiry:

---

25. Since *BH* is a characteristic proposition for the propensity distribution pr_{BH}, and likewise for *BT* and pr_{BT}, we have $pr_{BT}(BH) = 0$; $pr_{BT}(q \& BH) = 0$; $pr_{BH}(BH) = 1$; $pr_{BH}(q \& BH) = pr_{BH}(q)$. This then follows from the previous characterization of the mixture, providing appropriate probabilities are non-zero.

26. See the discussion of objectification in R. Jeffrey, *The Logic of Decision* (New York: Macmillan, 1965), and compare J. M. Keynes, *A Treatise on Probability*, ch. 24.

The order of nature, as perceived at first glance, presents at every instant a chaos followed by another chaos. We must decompose each chaos into single facts. . . . The extent and minuteness of observation which may be requisite, and the degree of decomposition to which it may be necessary to carry the mental analysis, depend on the particular purpose in view. (*A System of Logic*, 8th ed., bk. 3, ch. 7, p. 248)

Suppose we amplify our previous example. Which coin was chosen, the one biased toward heads or the one biased toward tails, depended on whether a red or black ball was drawn at random from an urn. The urn had either 80 percent black and 20 percent red or equal numbers of red and black. To get the "objective" probability of heads on the next toss, do I decompose with respect to the composition of the urn or with respect to the bias of the coin actually chosen? It depends on where my interests lie. Both are respectable objective probabilities.

We should also remember that "unknown objective probabilities" in which we have an interest may not always be probabilities of an effect; they may be probabilities of a cause. "Doctor, what are the chances that I have the disease?" "If the test comes out positive, the chances that you have it are about 60 percent; if negative, 45 percent." We could, of course, illustrate the nonuniqueness of decomposition further by chains of symptoms, as in the last paragraph we considered chains of causes. In this connection, it is worth remarking that testimony from a reliable observer is, in principle, no different from the results of a laboratory test and should be treated as a probabilistic symptom or sign.

The rich variety of pragmatically conditioned objective probabilities is, I think, a fact of life. The situation may appear messy to some, but the complexity of the facts should not be denied out of compulsive neatness. Still, there are some things that make the situation a bit neater than it at first appears. We suggested in the last section that *propensities* should be probability values that are *highly resilient*. Suppose that an objectified probability value (e.g., the probability of heads on the next toss on the hypothesis of a two-to-one bias toward heads, $pr_{BH}(H) =$

2/3) is highly resilient over a set of sentences (e.g., witch put a spell on the coin, coin came up heads on the last flip, man betting on heads is a steady loser, barometer is rising, gypsy said to bet on heads) in the objectified distribution (in pr_{BH}). Then that probability value will be approximately the same in probability distributions as we get from that distribution by objectifying with respect to those sentences. *Resiliency is a measure of invariance under further objectification.* This helps explain how scientific laws can be *saying* something, notwithstanding the nonuniqueness of the objectification process. The law says: "If a physical system is in state F, then the probability that it has property P is a." This tells us that for a canonical name (e.g., 32) *in the objective probability distribution corresponding to the exemplification of the antecedent ($pr_{F \text{ on } 32}$) the probability of the exemplification of the consequent is approximately a, and remains approximately a upon further objectification* (via the sentences in the domain of resiliency).[27] This account requires that probabilistic scientific laws carry with them an intended domain of resiliency. This is true both in classical statistical mechanics and in quantum mechanics. It is also true of the propensities that figure in games of chance, although the intentions are here a bit less clear-cut. (In games of chance, the pragmatics of the situation are economically based. The probabilities are supposed to be invariant over the factors of any gambling system that the player might devise. At the gaming table, the function of resiliency is to prevent cheating. The underlying determinism of the process is unimportant, since the gambler has no way of utilizing it for prediction.) It is, after all, the relative invariance of the probabilities that occur in probabilistic laws that enables them to function as stable contingent rules of inference.

It is no use trying to get a sense of maximally objective probability by objectifying on everything because, even if we had the resources to do so, it would only get us prob-

27. In the epistemic distribution of the man who regards the law as highly confirmed, the resiliency of $PR(G \text{ on } 32)$ being a, conditional on $(F \text{ on } 32)$, is high.

abilities of zero or one.[28] We could, however, do this:
Given some standard language for talking about what goes
on in regions of space-time, we could define *probability
maximally objectified according to causal antecedents* of
an event as its probability conditional on the complete description of the entire backward light cone of that event.[29]
Likewise, we can define *probability maximally objectified
according to signs, symptoms, and traces* by conditionalization on the description of the forward light cone. There
is at least one sense of *chance* for which the former concept provides a fair explication.[30] It is not the sense of Mill
or Venn, who conceived of chance as compatible with determinism, but rather the Greek sense in which chance
and determinism are contradictories. That ancient sense
of chance has again become interesting in the twentieth
century because of the development of quantum
mechanics. Indeed, given the quantum-mechanical state,
the quantum-mechanical probabilities of which it is a
foundation[31] are resilient over the entire backward light
cone.

   Still, it is not in the global conception of chance just
outlined that our ideas of objective probability find most
of their applications. We need not be as skeptical as Karl
Pearson:

> "All causes" might mean the whole past history of
> the universe, and what would happen if the universe
> started afresh from the same initial conditions, nobody
> knows, nor will anybody profitably stay to conjec-
> ture.[32]

to realize that more homely and less resilient propensities

28. By partitioning on maximal consistent sets of our language.
29. I here think of an event as represented by a sentence ascribing a
property to a space-time point. The property attaches to that sentence.
30. As suggested by David Lewis in "A Subjectivist's Guide to Objective Chance," in R. Jeffrey, ed., *Studies in Inductive Logic and Probability*, vol. 2 (Berkeley and Los Angeles: University of California Press,
1979).
31. The probabilities of getting a certain result conditional on per-
forming a certain measurement.
32. *The Grammar of Science* (London, 1892; reprint ed., New York:
Meridian, 1957), ch. 5, sec. 7.

also play an important role in our thinking. If a revolution occurred in physics and quantum mechanics were overthrown by a deterministic theory, we would still need a conception of propensity.[33]

IA5. Epistemic Probabilities and Relative Frequencies

Suppose we have a finite number of trials of an experiment. To keep things simple, consider four tosses of a coin. The proposition that half of the tosses come up heads—that the relative frequency of heads is one-half—is statable by enumerating the cases in which that is so:

> (H on 1 & H on 2 & T on 3 & T on 4) or
> (H on 1 & T on 2 & H on 3 & T on 4)
> etc.

Such statements, being truth-functional combinations of the elementary propositions about results of trials, are within the language over which probabilities are defined.[34]

We can, in consequence, ask a precise question about the evidential relation between relative frequencies and epistemic probabilities. *What is the epistemic probability of a trial exhibiting an outcome, conditional on the relative frequency of that outcome being some number,* a? (What is the probability of heads on trial 15, given that half the trials come up heads?) We cannot give a unique answer to the question in general, but in the case of *exchangeable sequences* the probability calculus dictates the answer that intuition desires:[35]

> $PR(H$ on n given that Relative Frequency of $H = a)$
> $= a$

33. For a different view, see H. Mellor, *The Matter of Chance* (Cambridge: Cambridge University Press, 1971).

34. If the language is closed under countably infinite disjunction and negation, then propositions ascribing limiting relative frequencies to outcomes in infinite sequences of trials are expressible. See R. Jeffrey, "Probability Measures and Integrals," in R. Carnap and R. Jeffrey, *Studies in Inductive Logic and Probability* (Berkeley and Los Angeles: University of California Press, 1971).

35. See appendix 1.

For an exchangeable sequence of trials, on the sole evidence of a statement of the relative frequency of an outcome, we take that relative frequency as our probability that the outcome will be exhibited on a trial.

In connection with the last section, this suggests that we might be interested in decomposing our epistemic probability distribution into "objective" probability distributions according to the relative frequencies of outcomes. In the example of the coin tossed four times, we have four possible objective relative-frequency distributions corresponding to conditionalization on the relative frequency of heads being 0, 1/4, 1/2, or 1. *If we start with an exchangeable sequence of trials* in the epistemic distribution, then the relation between relative frequency and probability in the "objective" distributions is even more intimate. *In these distributions, the probability of an outcome on a trial is the relative frequency of the outcome* (the relative frequency that that distribution gives probability 1). So, for example, the objective relative-frequency distribution corresponding to the relative frequency of heads being 1/2 makes the probability of heads on trial n (any trial) equal to 1/2.

This is a striking fact, and one might be tempted by it to speculate that the *real* meaning of objective probability is relative frequency. Such a speculation is, on the face of it, overenthusiastic, since the results just mentioned do require the hypothesis of exchangeability and furthermore only equate objective probability and relative frequency for one particular type of proposition, the probability that a certain trial has a certain outcome. A more modest hypothesis is that, under conditions of exchangeability, the use of relative frequency to factor out objective probability distributions always accords with our intuitive notions of objective probability, or propensity.

This modest hypothesis is, however, false. Consider our case of the coin that is either biased toward heads two to one, or similarly biased toward tails. The coin will be flipped four times, and we assume that the flips are (objectively) independent. We then have two *objective propensity distributions* pr_{BH} and pr_{BT}. Neither of these is identical to any of the objective relative-frequency distributions, since in each of the propensity distributions each of the possibilities regarding the relative frequency of heads receives a positive probability different from zero of one. Furthermore, by hypothesis, in each objective propensity distribution the flips are *independent*. But in the objective relative-frequency distribution corresponding to half of the tosses coming up heads, the probability of heads on 3 is one-half, but the probability of tails on 3, *given* heads on 1 and 2, is one! The tosses are *not independent* in the objective relative-frequency distributions. Here epistemic probability can be represented as the expectation of objective propensity or as the expectation of objective relative frequency, but it does not follow that they are the same. Confusing the two, in cases like this, is known as the *gambler's fallacy*! We know that the decomposition of epistemic probabilities is not unique, so the moral here is just that decomposition according to relative frequency does not always give us the most suitable variety of "objective" probability.

It should be noted, however, that the peculiarities of the objective relative-frequency distributions that I have just pointed out diminish as the number of trials increases. Decomposing an *infinite* sequence of *exchangeable* trials into objective relative-frequency distributions has the consequence that in each objective relative-frequency distribution the trials are *independent*.[36] So *if* the propensities in question are supposed to be independent, as in coin tossing, an objective relative-frequency distribution may be a fair facsimile of the propensities. Just how close the relationship is, in this special case, calls for a discussion of the philosophical significance of laws of large numbers.

IA6. PROPENSITIES, RELATIVE FREQUENCIES, AND LAWS OF LARGE NUMBERS

Suppose you have a fair coin that you intend to flip. If you flip it once the relative frequency of heads in that "sequence" of one flip will be one or zero. If you flip it five

36. See appendix 1. This is De Finetti's theorem.

times, you would still not be too surprised to get all heads or all tails. But you would be quite surprised at such a result on 100,000 tosses. Indeed, on such a large number of trials you would expect with a high degree of confidence that the relative frequency of heads would be close to one-half. Such intuitions receive precise formulation and backing via laws of large numbers:

> If we have an *independent* sequence of trials of an experiment such that the probability of an outcome (e.g., heads) is the same on every trial,[37] then no matter how high a probability (short of one) we desire for the relative frequency of an outcome to approximate its probability of occurrence on a trial, and no matter how closely we specify that the one number approximate the other (short of specifying that they be equal), there is always a large enough number of trials such that the probability of the relative frequency getting as close as you wanted to the probability, and staying that close for as many further trials as you please, is as high as you wanted.

So, for instance, with the fair coin there is a number of flips such that the probability that the relative frequency of heads within those flips is within .00000001 of one-half and will stay within those limits for the next billion flips is at least .999999. This is the *strong law of large numbers*. Its statement is a bit tedious, but the details are important (e.g., the omission of either of the parenthetical qualifications would render the statement false).

The strong law of large numbers gives us a strong relation between certain cases of propensity (independent and identically distributed trials) and relative frequency. But it would be an overestimation of this result to claim that propensities *are* relative frequencies, or that propensities must be equal to relative frequencies, or even that, in a large number of trials, propensities *must be close to* relative frequencies.

37. The trials are said to be identically distributed. A sequence of independent and identically distributed trials is called *Bernoullian*. Note that Bernoullian sequences are a fortiori exchangeable.

There is more than one chance process going on in the world![38] Suppose m coins are each flipped independently n times. By choosing n big enough, we can, according to the law of large numbers, make it highly unlikely, for *each* coin, that the relative frequency of heads for *that* coin will differ much from 1/2. But it does not follow that it is highly unlikly that *any* coin have a relative frequency of heads differing appreciably from 1/2. On the contrary, for any fixed n, we can find an m such that the probability *that some coin comes up all heads* is as high as you please (short of one). Indeed, this also follows from the strong law of large numbers if we think now of flipping a coin n times as a trial, and flipping another coin n times as another trial in a supersequence and getting all heads as an outcome with a probability on a trial of $1/2^n$. Picking m (the number of supertrials) large enough will make it highly likely that the relative frequency of All Heads coins in the supersequence is about $1/2^n$, and a fortiori that at least one coin comes up all heads. *There is nothing more probable than that something improbable will happen, but it is impossible that something impossible should happen. Attempts to use the law of large numbers to defend the thesis that probability is relative frequency all slide from improbability to impossibility at a conveniently chosen crucial point.*

The fallacies of misinterpreting the law of large numbers as a justification of the frequency interpretation of probability can be disguised by artfully taking limits, but they do not thereby disappear. If we extend our language so that we can talk in it about limiting relative frequencies in an infinite sequence of trials and make a few assumptions about limiting probabilities, we can state what appears to be a more powerful version of the law of large numbers: the probability that, in a given sequence of independent and identically distributed trials, the limiting relative frequency will either fail to exist or diverge by some positive real number from the probability of the out-

38. Essentially the same argument is advanced in P. Railton, ''A Deductive-Nomological Model of Probabilistic Explanation.''

come is infinitesimal.[39] Then, if our coin is flipped an infinite number of times, the probability that the *limiting*
relative frequency fails to be one-half is infinitesimal. All
that is needed to complete the proof that for the sorts of
sequences and statements at issue, propensity equals
limiting relative frequency, is the principle that *infinitesimal propensity implies impossibility.* However, adding
this principle to the foregoing renders the entire scheme
inconsistent. To see this, we need only notice that the assumptions that get the striking version of the strong law of
large numbers give us infinitesimal probability not only
for the outcome sequence All Heads, *but for each other
definite sequence of outcomes as well.*[40] But the coin has
to do something! There is nothing more probable than that
something improbable will happen, but it is impossible
that something impossible should happen. Small probability, even infinitesimally small probability, does not
mean impossibility. Then even if, for each process, the
propensity for a divergence between propensity and relative frequency is infinitesimal, it hardly follows that the
propensity for a divergence for some process, somewhere
in the world, is infinitesimal. But this is just what those
who wish to turn the law of large numbers into a
philosophical analysis of propensity must assume.

It is perhaps worth noting that recent attempts to construe propensities as modalized relative frequencies *only
make things worse* in this regard.[41] Thus, suppose that
someone suggests that we read: "the coin has a propensity
of one-half to come up heads" as "in any physically possible world in which the coin is flipped an infinite number
of times, the limiting relative frequency of heads is one-
half" (thereby building in a kind of necessity and at the

39. By *infinitesimal* I mean less than any positive real number. For
there to be infinitesimals other than zero, we have to introduce numbers
other than the standard reals. See appendix 4.

40. If we forget about the possibility of introducing nonstandard reals, the assumption in question is sigma additivity.

41. See H. Kyberg's review article, "Propensities and Probabilities,"
British Journal for the Philosophy of Science 25 (1974):358–75, and B.
van Fraassen's "Relative Frequencies," *Synthese* 34:133–66.

same time finding large numbers of trials in possible worlds for cases where they do not exist in the actual world). If, as I have argued, we are to expect some divergences of limiting relative frequency from propensity in this world, how much more are we to expect some divergence in the field of all physically possible worlds? On the hypothesis that the coin has a propensity of one-half to come up heads on a trial and that the trials are independent, *each infinite sequence of outcomes is equally possible. If we look at all physically possible worlds, we will find them all,* including the outcome sequence composed of all heads. This unavoidable fact makes the error of a whole family of frequency-in-a-possible-world views of propensity crystal clear. The correct reading of the law of large numbers is not that propensity is modalized or hypothetical frequency, but rather that, in an important class of cases that fulfill the conditions for the law of large numbers, *propensity involves a strong propensity to display a relative frequency.*

IA7. EPISTEMIC PROBABILITIES, PROPENSITIES, AND RELATIVE FREQUENCIES. OBJECTIVE, SUBJECTIVE, AND EXTENSIONAL RANDOMNESS.

Epistemic probabilities can be thought of as expectations of objective probabilities, which, if they meet the right requirements of resiliency or physical randomness, may be dignified by the name *propensities.* Epistemic probabilities can also, in the case of exchangeable sequences, be thought of as expectations of objective relative-frequency distributions. In the case of finite sequences of trials, the trials of these objective relative-frequency distributions are not statistically independent, but in the case of an infinite sequence of trials they are. *If* the propensities in question generate an infinite sequence of independent trials, the propensity distribution may differ at most infinitesimally from the objective relative-frequency distribution. This fact is explained by the strong law of large numbers, which, however, must not be misinterpreted as implying the identity, even in these special cases, of propensity and relative frequency.

There is a generalization of the law of large numbers, due to De Finetti, which will allow us to complete this survey of the interrelations between epistemic probability, propensity, and relative frequency. Suppose that we have a sequence of trials that are only exchangeable, rather than independent. Then it can still be shown that as the number of trials approaches infinity the probability approaches one that the relative frequency converges to a limiting relative frequency, but in this case it cannot be shown that the relative frequency of an outcome approaches the probability of that outcome.

We can see what is behind this fact by considering the exchangeable epistemic distribution that we get by averaging the two independent distributions representing the coin being biased two-to-one toward heads or two-to-one toward tails. The epistemic probability of heads on a trial is one-half. The epistemic probability approaches one that the relative frequency converges to a limit, but not that it converges to one-half, rather that it converges to either one-third or two-thirds. One can say, then, that when the epistemic probability distribution gives an infinite exchangeable sequence of trials, then the epistemic probability approaches one that the relative frequency approaches the single case probability in one of the relative frequency distributions of which it is a mixture.

In the case of exchangeable epistemic probabilities and independent propensities, we have a tissue of probabilistic connections between propensity, epistemic probability, and relative frequency. The strength of these connections increases with the number of trials, and it approaches one as the number of trials goes to infinity. Still, the connections are probabilistic and not deductive, and they have only been established under certain conditions. We may, and typically do, get our propensity distribution by conditioning on something other than the limiting relative frequency (e.g., on some physical properties of the experimental arrangement). Propensities involve propensities for relative frequencies. Relative frequencies constitute evidence for propensities, but the two concepts are distinct.

The hallmark of propensities for me is high resiliency

or physical randomness. The achievement of this property is a guiding principle in the decomposition of our epistemic probabilities into possible objective probabilities, and it is part of standard scientific procedure to follow this principle. A sequence of trials which displays a limiting relative frequency of an outcome need not be random, so my conception is more closely related to von Mises's notion of a collective, or extensional random sequence than to the bare notion of limiting relative frequency. Indeed, we have objective, epistemic, and extensional notions of randomness as counterparts of objective, epistemic, and extensional (relative frequency) notions of probability. There is even a "law of large numbers" relating objective and extensional randomness, roughly to the effect that random sampling has a high propensity to produce random sequences.[42] And like independence of trials, physical randomness also leaves its mark on an epistemic distribution which is a mixture of propensity distributions.

If high resiliency is an important part of what makes propensities propensities and what makes statistical laws lawlike, then it should provide some insight into the lawlikeness of universal laws and into the nature of a number of key philosophical concepts connected with laws. These are the issues I propose to explore in the rest of this book.

42. See P. Martin-Lof, "The Definition of Random Sequences," *Information and Control* 9 (1966):602–19.

IB Universal Laws as Limiting Cases of Statistical Laws

If universal laws are regarded as limiting cases of statistical laws, then the considerations of approximate invariance (resiliency) introduced in chapter IA allow some much-discussed problems concerning their confirmation to be viewed in a new light. A universal law may be thought of as asserting that everything within the scope of its quantifier has a propensity of one to not be a counterexample. "All ravens are black" would thus be thought of as "Everything has a propensity of one to not be a nonblack raven" or, equivalently, "everything has a propensity of one to be either black, or not a raven, or both." The centrality of the material conditional to this account may lead some to take a different limiting case—"Every raven has a propensity of one to be black"—as the preferred paraphrase of "All ravens are black." On the surface, these two accounts appear to be quite different, with the material conditional account being notorious for making laws easier to confirm (in disturbing ways) than the conditional probability account. Nevertheless, it turns out that *if resiliency requirements are taken stringently enough*, the fact that a law is well confirmed on the first reading will entail that it is on the second also. There might also be some temptation to insert a modal necessity operator into the sentence, but I shall argue that modal requirements are also present already in requirements of resiliency. The shift in viewpoint to considerations of resiliency reveals the common ground for prima facie incompatible accounts of laws.

Throughout this section, instead of writing "the resiliency of $Pr(p)$ being 1," I will simply write "the resiliency of p." I will assume that we have names for outcomes which function only as labels—all descriptive information as to order and so forth being built into predicates—and that this makes it plausible that for unexamined outcomes we have "symmetry" or "exchangeability," that is to say, invariance of the probabilities under permutation of the names. Given such names for unexamined outcomes, and a list of factors $F_1 \ldots F_m$ over which resiliency is to be evaluated, we can form an associated n-instantial language by choosing n names $\alpha_1 \ldots \alpha_n$,[1] combining them with the factors in all possible ways to form atomic sentences, and closing under Boolean operations &, $\vee$, $\sim$. Often only the simplest case of the 1-instantial language will be treated explicitly, but the general case should be kept in mind.

For some of the most startling results of this section, the instantial language used to evaluate a law must include in its list of generating factors the predicates of the law itself, the leading idea being roughly that for "All ravens are black" to be well confirmed, "If it's a raven, it's black" should be resilient over "It's a raven." Thus the instantial language relevant to "All Fs are Gs" would include as sentences: $F\alpha \& G\alpha$, $F\alpha \& \sim G\alpha$, etc. In such cases, in evaluating the resiliency of $F\alpha \supset G\alpha$, we must invoke the restriction mentioned in passing in the last section:

Resiliency $(F\alpha \supset G\alpha) = 1 - \mathrm{Max}_i |1 - \Pr(F\alpha \supset G\alpha$ given $p_i)|^2$ where the p_is are propositions of the instantial language *compatible with $F\alpha \supset G\alpha$* and its negation.

We should be clear at the onset, however, that inclusion of the predicates F and G in the list of generating factors makes high resiliency of $F\alpha \supset G\alpha$ *much* harder to attain.[3] This makes all the more interesting the fact that prima facie plausible constraints on the confirmation of "All Fs are Gs" *require* high resiliency of $F\alpha \supset G\alpha$ over just such an instantial language, although it renders the philosophical moral of the story more problematical.

---

1. Which n names are chosen makes no difference because of exchangeability.

2. Or, more simply, Minimum $_i \Pr(F \supset G$ given $p_i)$.

3. But not impossible. If $\Pr(F\alpha \& \sim G\alpha) = 0$ and every other atom of the instantial language has non-zero probability, then resiliency of $F\alpha \supset G\alpha = 1$.

IB1. The Paradox of Provisional Acceptance

Why do they never explain why we continue to use laws that we know to be false.

Feyerabend
"Against Method"

Feyerabend's remark suggests that what is important about a law for scientific practice is something other than probability of truth. I believe that there is an argument here that is to be taken seriously—one that cannot be disposed of with a few epsilons—although it need not drive us quite so far as intellectual anarchism. The argument that I have in mind was perhaps stated most forcefully by Ramsey. It turns on what I shall call the *paradox of provisional acceptance* of laws.

When we look back over the history of science, we see a pattern of laws being confirmed and accepted, serving well for a time, but eventually breaking down when confronted with new domains of experiment and observation and finally being superseded and replaced by more adequate laws. This is not to say that the old law is then regarded as rubbish! It may be and often is regarded as a useful approximation within a limited domain of phenomena. But, taken in full generality, it is regarded as false. Accordingly, when we accept a law now, we do so with the expectation that it will eventually be superseded, that we will eventually uncover a domain of experiment and observation where there are counterinstances to it. We say that we accept the law "only provisionally." But what does this mean? If we believe that there *are* counterinstances to the law, whether they have been discovered yet or not, we must believe that the law is false! Belief that "All Fs are Gs" has a counterinstance is belief that there is (was or will be) an F which isn't a G. Thus belief in a law, in the sense in which we can be said to believe our best scientific theories, cannot be belief in its truth and indeed must be consistent with belief in its falsity. Likewise, a "well-confirmed" scientific law cannot simply be one which is probably true. It should be consistent to hold both that a law is well confirmed and that its probability of truth is low. (One might hold that the law "All *F*s are *G*s" is not properly rendered as "There is no *F* which is not a *G*," but rather by some modalized version thereof; however, clearly this only makes the problem worse.)

The premise seems so mundane and the conclusion so surprising that the argument calls for a closer look. The generalization about the history of science with which I started is not very controversial. Simply put, it is this: "Time after time we had a law or theory which worked very well, and then new considerations led us to believe that it was wrong." This modest observation in no way depends on radical skepticism regarding comparability of scientific theories and progress in science. It is quite consistent with a belief in the principle of correspondence, with the view that there *is* progress in science and that the old rejected theory is regarded from the vantage point of the new as a reasonable approximation within some limited domain (but note that it may be *wildly* inaccurate outside that domain). The historical claim is there solely to persuade you that it is *reasonable*, when we accept a law now, to accept it with the expectation that it will eventually be superseded.

David Bohm's *Causality and Chance in Modern Physics* is a persuasive argument from the history of science to this conclusion. Bohm goes further. He argues that we should accept a *metaphysical principle* of the qualitative infinity of nature, which has as a consequence that this progression of theories will never stop. I would not want to go this far. Suppose we found a unified theory which explained everything we know beautifully. Suppose such a theory handled everything we confronted it with for the next hundred years, or the next thousand. Would we not then be justified in believing that it was the ultimate theory? Would we not then be justified in believing that its laws were *true*? I do not see why not. But we should be clear that all that is required for the argument is that *sometimes* it is reasonable to accept a theory or regard it as well confirmed and at the same time believe or think it probable that a counterinstance to it exists.

In fact, I think that we are living in such a time now. Near the end of the nineteenth century, most scientists may have believed that truth had been attained. But at present most physicists regard even our best scientific theories as transitional.

The problem, then, is to find a sense of provisional acceptance or confirmation which helps clarify this irritating epistemological situation. Carnap came to this problem from a different direction. What seemed to him plausible confirmation functions all gave the result that, in an infinite universe, all universal generalizations have probability zero on finite evidence. Carnap was thus led a priori to the conclusion that we have reached a posteriori, that a law may be regarded as well confirmed while its probability of truth is low. The internal difficulties of Carnap's inducti·ve logic need not concern us here. In fact, Hintikka has shown, using methods quite in the spirit of Carnap, how to construct confirmation functions which *do* allow universal generalizations to achieve respectable probabilities on finite evidence. But Carnap's response to the problem is of interest:

One might perhaps think at first that h is the law in question, hence a universal sentence l of the form: "For every space-time point x, if such and such conditions are fulfilled at x, then such and such is the case at x". I think, however, that the engineer is chiefly interested not in this sentence l, which speaks about an immense number, perhaps an infinite number, of instances dispersed through all time and space, but rather in one instance of l or a relatively small number of instances. When he says that the law is very reliable, he does not mean to say that he is willing to bet that among the billions of billions, or an infinite number, of instances to which the law applies there is not one counterinstance, but merely that this bridge will not be a counterinstance, or that among all bridges which he will construct during his lifetime there will be no counterinstance. Thus h is not the law l itself but only a prediction concerning one instance or a relatively small number of instances. Therefore, what is called the reliability of a law is measured not by the degree of confirmation of the law itself but that of one or several instances. This suggests the subsequent definitions. They refer, for the sake of simplicity, to just one instance; the case of several, say, one hundred, instances can then easily be judged likewise. Let e be any non-L-false, nongeneral sentence. Let l be a simple law (D37-I) of the form $(i_k)(M_i)$. Then we understand by the *instance confirmation* of l on the evidence e, in symbols '$c^*_i (1, e)$', the degree of confirmation, on the evidence e, of the hypothesis that a new individual not mentioned in e fulfills the law l:

14             $c^*_i (l, e) = Df C^* (h, e),$

where h is an instance of M_i formed by substituting for i_k an individual constant not occurring in e.

The second concept, now to be defined seems in many cases to represent still more accurately what is vaguely meant by the reliability of a law l. We suppose here that l has the frequently used conditional form mentioned earlier: '$(x)(Mx \supset M'x)$' (e.g., "all swans are white"). By the *qualified-instance confirmation* of the law that all swans are white we mean the degree of confirmation for the hypothesis h' that the next swan to be observed will likewise be white. The difference between the hypothesis h used previously for the instance confirmation and the hypothesis h' just described consists in the fact that the latter concerns an individual which is already qualified as fulfilling the condition M.[4]

In seeking to locate the relevant measure of confirmation of a law on the instantial level, Carnap is acting in accordance with intuitions that Ramsey expressed before the special problems with Carnap's confirmation functions ever arose. One of the reasons that "variable hypotheticals" (our simplest laws, e.g., "All men are mortal") are not to be thought of as infinite conjuntions is that:

---

4. *Logical Foundations of Probability*, 2d ed. (Chicago: University of Chicago Press, 1962).

The relevant degree of certainty is the certainty of the particular case, or of a finite set of particular cases; not of an infinite number which we never use, and of which we couldn't be certain at all.[5]

The move to the instantial level, to instance confirmation, qualified instance confirmation, or some other instantial measure of the "well-confirmedness" of a law, provides the only reasonable explanation I know of for the paradox of provisional acceptance of laws. When a law is provisionally accepted or regarded as well confirmed, the evidence is such that for each instance it is probable that the application of the law to that instance will be successful. This is quite consistent with believing that it is probable that some item is a counterexample, although it entails that there is no item such that we believe it probable that *it* is a counterexample. We can believe that the extensional counterpart of the law is *false*, and yet believe that it is reasonable to apply it, as if true, to individual instances, since each such application is overwhelmingly likely to be successful. Thus Ramsey says: "It [a law] expresses an inference that we are at any time prepared to make, not a belief of the primary sort," and "Variable hypotheticals or causal laws form the system with which the speaker meets the future. . . . Variable hypotheticals are not judgments but rules for judging 'If I meet a ϕ, I shall regard it as a χ.' "

Following Ramsey, Carnap, and Bohm cautiously, we might draw this modest conclusion from the paradox of provisional acceptance: at least one important sense of "well-confirmed" should be explicated at the level of the instantial language.

IB2. THE PREDICTIVE FUNCTION OF LAWS

Ramsey believes that "variable hypotheticals are not judgments, but rules for judging 'If I meet a ϕ I shall regard it as a χ.' " Not everyone would agree that laws are

5. *The Foundations of Mathematics and Other Logical Essays,* (London: Routledge & Kegan Paul, 1931).

not judgments, but most would, I think, agree that laws must *at least* fulfill the function Ramsey ascribes to them. That is, if we have a law, "All Fs are Gs," which is well confirmed, and then run across a new individual, a, which we determine to have F, we will apply the law and conclude that a has the property G as well. This is not the only way that laws are used in making predictions, but it is an especially natural and important way and it should hold up if anything does. Let us call the function of supporting such inferences the *paradigm predictive function* of laws. If the effect of learning of a new individual, a, that it has the property F is correctly represented by conditionalization of Fa, then, in order to fulfill its *paradigm predictive function*, a law, "All Fs are Gs," should be well confirmed in a high degree only if the probabilities are such that conditionalization on Fa would lead to a high probability for Ga; that is, only if the conditional probability $Pr(Ga$ given $Fa)$ is high. This translates into the following *condition of adequacy* on a numerical measure of well-confirmedness of laws, C:

Criterion I.

C(All Fs are Gs) $\leq Pr(Ga$ given $Fa)$ (for "new" a)[6]

This condition of adequacy on a measure of well-confirmedness of laws is so natural that it may be somewhat surprising that the prima facie natural measure $Pr(Fa \supset Ga)$,[7] and even the stronger requirements of $Pr(x)(Fx \supset Gx)$, need not fulfill it. This weakness shows up dramatically in the case of laws with *vacuous antecedents*. It is an elementary algebraic fact that the probability of the universally quantified material conditional must be at least as great as the probability that its antecedent is vacuous $[Pr(x)(Fx \supset Gx) \geq Pr(x)(\sim Fx)]$. Likewise, on the instantial level, we have the algebraic truth that the instance confirmation of "All Fs are Gs," $Pr(Fa \supset Ga)$, must be at least as great as the instance confirmation of "Every-

---

6. That is to say, in Carnap's terminology, that the measure of well-confirmedness of a law should be a lower bound on the *qualified instance confirmation* of the law; a high value for well-confirmedness should guarantee an equally high value for qualified instance confirmation and thus for $Pr(Ga)$ after Fa has been learned with certainty.

7. Carnap's instance confirmation.

thing is a non-F" $Pr(\sim Fa)$. Thus evidence for the vacuousness of the law in the strong sense of high $Pr(x)(\sim Fx)$ or the weak sense of high instance confirmation of "Everything is a non-F" is at least as good evidence for the law in the sense of high probability of the extensional counterpart and high instance confirmation respectively.

The predictive force, $Pr(Ga \text{ given } Fa)$, of a law is not, however, enhanced by evidence of the vacuousness of the law. Evidence for the vacuousness of a law may render the probability that we will encounter an F miniscule, but the qualified instance confirmation of the law, being a conditional probability, depends only on the *ratio*, within that miniscule probability, of $Pr(Fa \& Ga)/Pr(Fa)$. Thus $Pr(\sim Fa)$ may be as high as you please (short of one) while $Pr(Ga \text{ given } Fa)$ is as low as you please. The relation between the instance confirmation and the qualified instance confirmation of the law is summarized in the following equation: the instance confirmation, $Pr(Fa \supset Ga)$, equals its qualified instance confirmation, $Pr(Ga \text{ given } Fa)$, times the probability that the instance instantiates the antecedent, $Pr(Fa)$ *plus* the probability that the instance does not instantiate the antecedent, $Pr(\sim Fa)$:

$$Pr(Fa \supset Ga) = [Pr(Ga \text{ given } Fa) Pr(Fa)] + Pr(\sim Fa)$$

Thus it is clear that instance confirmation and even probability of the universally quantified material conditional cannot do justice to the paradigm predictive function of laws. If I believe strongly that there are no charmed quarks, I may thereby award high instance confirmation to "All charmed quarks exceed the speed of light," and if my belief is strong enough I may even regard the associated universally quantified material conditional as probable. But I may nevertheless regard as low the conditional probability that some particle with which I am unacquainted, $Ralph$, is traveling faster than the speed of light, given that Ralph is a charmed quark. I may *by no means* be disposed to predict that Ralph is exceeding the speed of light if I become convinced that Ralph is a charmed quark.

In such cases, it is clear where our intuitions lie. They lie with preserving the paradigm predictive function of laws, rather than with considering vacuous universal generalizations as law. Thus the following remarks of Nagel in *The Structure of Science*:

> An unrestricted universal conditional may be true, simply because it is vacuously true (i.e., nothing whatever satisfies its antecedent clause). But if such a conditional is accepted for this reason alone, it is un-likely that anyone will number it among the laws of nature. For example, if we assume (as we have good reason to) that there are no unicorns, the rules of logic require us also to accept as true that all unicorns are fleet of foot. Despite this, however, even those familiar with formal logic will hesitate to classify this latter statement as a law of nature—especially since logic also requires us to accept as true, on the basis of the very same initial assumption, that all unicorns are slow runners. Most people would in fact regard it as at best a mild joke were a universal conditional labeled a law because it is vacuously true. The reason for this lies in good part in the uses which are normally made of laws: to explain phenomena and other laws, to pre-dict events, and in general to serve as instruments for making inference in inquiry. But if a universal condi-tional is accepted on the ground that it is vacuously true, there is nothing to which it can be applied, so that it cannot perform the inferential functions which laws are expected to perform.[8]

Although Nagel's discussion is from within a framework of deduction and truth, the preceding shows that it takes on even more force within a framework of confirmation and probability.

A few more considerations will emphasize, from slightly different angles, the importance of criterion I. Suppose, first, that contrary to criterion I a law could be well confirmed while its qualified instance confirmation was low. But if the qualified instance confirmation $Pr(Ga$ given $Fa)$ is low, then $Pr(\sim Ga$ given $Fa)$ is high. Thus, if

8. *The Structure of Science* (New York: Harcourt Brace, 1961), pp. 59–60.

we merely found something that satisfied the antecedent of the law (Fa), assimilation of this knowledge (by conditionalization on Fa) would render a counterexample to the law (Fa & $\sim Ga$) probable and thus disconfirm the law. Such a "law" would wear its dependence on vacuity shamelessly on its face; *mere discovery of an instance to which it applied would disconfirm it!*[9]

Another phenomenon that points up the oddness of "confirmation by vacuity" and the importance of the paradigm predictive function of laws has to do with the confirmational relation of a law to its contrary. If a law is confirmed vacuously, then so is its contrary. If $Pr(x)(\sim Fx)$ is high, not only $(x)(Fx \supset Gx)$ but also $(x)(Fx \supset \sim Gx)$ must have probability at least as high; if $Pr(\sim Fa)$ is high then the instance confirmation of both "All Fs are Gs" and "All Fs are not Gs" must be at least as high.

The oddness of holding both a law and its contrary to be well confirmed has been widely noticed in connection with Hempel's studies on confirmation. In *Fact, Fiction and Forecast*, Goodman writes:

> New difficulties promptly appear from other directions, however. One is the infamous paradox of the ravens. The statement that a given object, say this piece of paper, is neither black nor a raven confirms the hypothesis that all non-black things are non-ravens. But this hypothesis is logically equivalent to the

---

9. In calling Fa & $\sim Ga$ a counterexample to the law (which it certainly is intuitively), I am assuming a probabilistic constraint on "well-confirmedness," i.e.:

IA: $C(\text{All } Fs \text{ are } Gs) \leq 1 - Pr(Fb \& Gb)$ (for *any* b)

Now let Pr_f be a probability distribution gotten from Pr_i by conditionalizing on Fa (for some "new" a). We formulate the following principle of "independence from vacuity":

IB: $C_f(\text{All } Fs \text{ are } Gs) \geq C_i(\text{All } Fs \text{ are } Gs)$

which says that discovering an instance to which the law applies does not diminish the well-confirmedness of the law. (There is no reason why it should augment the well-confirmedness of a law either, so presumably IB would still be plausible with an equality.) Now IA and IB together imply criterion I. For suppose, contrary to criterion I, that C_i (All Fs are Gs) $> Pr_i$ (Ga given Fa). $Pr_f(Fa \& \sim Ga) = 1 - Pr_f$ (Ga given Fa) but, by IA, C_f (All Fs are Gs $\leq 1 - Pr_f(Fa \& \sim Ga)$; thus C_f (All Fs are Gs) $\leq Pr_i$ (Ga given Fa), so C_f (All Fs are Gs) $< C_i$ (All Fs are Gs), contrary to IB.

hypothesis that all ravens are black. Hence we arrive at the unexpected conclusion that the statement that a given object is neither black nor a raven confirms the hypothesis that all ravens are black. The prospect of being able to investigate ornithological theories without going out in the rain is so attractive that we know there must be a catch in it. The trouble this time, however, lies not in faulty definition, but in tacit and illicit reference to evidence not stated in our example. Taken by itself, the statement that the given object is neither black nor a raven confirms the hypothesis that everything that is not a raven is not black as well as the hypothesis that everything that is not black is not a raven. We tend to ignore the former hypothesis because we know it to be false from abundant other evidence—from all the familiar things that are not ravens but are black. But we are required to assume that no such evidence is available. Under this circumstance, even a much stronger hypothesis is also obviously confirmed; that nothing is either black or a raven. In the light of this confirmation of the hypothesis that there are no ravens; it is no longer surprising that under the artificial restrictions of the example, the hypothesis that all ravens are black is also confirmed. And the prospects for indoor ornithology vanish when we notice that under these same conditions the contrary hypothesis that no ravens are black is equally well confirmed.[10]

Taking up Goodman's line of thought, Scheffler introduces the notion of *selective confirmation.* A statement selectively confiirms a law when it "accords with it but not also with its contrary (in the extreme case violating its contrary). It may be further suggested that *confirming* a hypothesis typically involves favoring it in this way as against a contrary one)." Scheffler defends his hypothesis that the correct meaning of "confirmation" is selective confirmation on familiar pragmatic grounds.[11] If "All ra-

10. *Fact, Fiction and Forecast,* 2d ed. (New York: Bobbs-Merrill, 1965).

11. *The Anatomy of Inquiry* (Indianapolis: Bobbs-Merrill, 1963).

vens are black" and "All ravens are not black" could both
be well confirmed at the same time, then what help would
the well-confirmedness of "All ravens are black" be in
predicting the color of a newly discovered raven? A measure of well-confirmedness which satisfies criterion I will
not, of course, allow both a law and its contrary to be well
confirmed. Such a measure may then be thought of as a
probabilistic generalization of Scheffler's idea of selective
confirmation.

The questions of the paradigm predictive function of
laws, the nonvacuous confirmation of laws, and the selective confirmation of laws vis-à-vis their contraries are different faces of the same issue. Taken together, the considerations surrounding this issue argue strongly for criterion I.

IB3. THE EQUIVALENCE CONDITION

Anyone who maintains that the well-confirmedness of a
law is different from the probability of the associated universal material conditional must provide an explanation
of why the confusion of the two causes so little trouble.[12]

After all, scientists do not generally make the nice distinction between a law and its associated universal material conditional that I have been urging. And yet they ap-
parently apply laws perfectly well, suffering no unhappy
consequences from their confusion. What this suggests
is that well-confirmedness of a law must in many respects
behave like a probability on its associated material
conditional. In particular, it suggests the following
equivalence condition:
   Criterion II.

> If two laws have logically equivalent associated
> universal material conditionals, then they are
> well confirmed to exactly the same degree.

Such a pragmatic argument for the equivalence condition is forcefully expressed by Hempel in "Studies in the
Logic of Confirmation":

---

12. I am not saying that it causes no trouble. I have just pointed out
some trouble that it causes. But why doesn't it cause more?

The results obtained call attention to the following condition which an adequately defined concept of confirmation should satisfy, and in light of which Nicod's criterion has to be rejected as inadequate:

Equivalence Condition: Whatever confirms (disconfirms) one of two equivalent sentences, also confirms (disconfirms) the other.

Fulfillment of this condition makes the confirmation of a hypothesis independent of the way in which it is formulated; and no doubt it will be conceded that this is a necessary condition for the adequacy of any proposed criterion of confirmation. Otherwise, the question as to whether certain data confirm a given hypothesis would have to be answered by saying: "That depends on which of the different equivalent formulations of the hypothesis is considered"—which appears absurd. Furthermore—and this is a more important point than an appeal to a feeling of absurdity—an adequate definition of confirmation will have to do justice to the way in which empirical hypotheses function in theoretical scientific contexts such as explanations and predictions; but when hypotheses are used for purposes of explanation or prediction, they serve as premises in a deductive argument whose conclusion is a description of the event to be explained or predicted. The deduction is governed by the principles of formal logic, and according to the latter, a deduction which is valid will remain so if some or all of the premises are replaced by different but equivalent statements; and indeed, a scientist will feel free, in any theoretical reasoning involving certain hypotheses, to use the latter in whichever of their equivalent formulations are most convenient for the development of his conclusions. But if we adopted a concept of confirmation which did not satisfy the equivalence condition, then it would be possible, and indeed necessary, to argue in certain cases that it was sound scientific procedure to base a prediction on a given hypothesis if formulated in a sentence S_1, because a good deal of confirming evidence had been found for S_1; but that it was altogether inadmissible to base the predic-

tion (say, for convenience of deduction) on an equivalent
formulation S_2, because no confirming evidence for S_2 was
available. Thus, the equivalence condition has to be regarded as a necessary condition for the adequacy of any
definition of confirmation.[13]

To what extent is it possible to resist Hempel's arguments? The first argument, that confirmation of the
hypothesis should be independent of the way in which it
is formulated, is by itself rather weak. It *assumes* that two
laws with logically equivalent universal material conditionals are different formulations of the *same* hypothesis.
This constitutes rather a persuasive definition of
"hypothesis." It, together with the natural assumption
that it is the hypothesis that we are confirming, effectively
begs the question.

But this line of defense runs afoul of Hempel's second
argument. The definition of hypothesis is not arbitrary or
capricious but rather is drawn from scientific practice. If
two laws have logically equivalent associated universal
material conditionals (we shall say that the laws are then
quasi-equivalents) and one is regarded as well confirmed,
the other is regarded as thereby equally well confirmed.
This attitude, Hempel maintains, is not merely an oddity
in scientists' behavior; rather it is deeply rooted in the deductive structure of scientific theory and the applications
of that theory to explanation and prediction.

It seems to me that the only possible defense against
this line of argument would be to dispute what Hempel
takes to be the facts of scientific practice; that is, to claim
that the hypothetico-deductive model of science and the
deductive-nomological models of scientific explanation
and prediction are fundamental misrepresentations of scientific practice. There is something to be said along these
lines, but not, I think, enough. It is true that only very old
and venerable scientific theories get axiomatized; that a
developing scientific theory, even one as mathematized as
physics, tends to have much more an inductive structure
and much less a deductive structure than consideration of

13. In *Aspects of Scientific Explanation and Other Essays in the Philosophy of Science* (New York: Free Press, 1965).

axiomatic paradigms would suggest; that much scientific explanation and prediction takes place in contexts which fall short of the deductive-nomological ideal. Much more could be said against an overly deductive view of the scientific enterprise. But, notwithstanding, I think that Hempel's point is basically a good one. If a scientist believes *qua* law that all sodium salts burn yellow, he will not shrink from believing its contrapositive, "Anything that does not burn yellow is no sodium salt," and using it, in the manner of the paradigm predictive argument, to predict of a sample that does not burn yellow that it is no sodium salt. Any scientist will regard "volume = k temperature/pressure" and "pressure = k temperature/volume" as mathematically equivalent formulations of the same law, confirmed to exactly the same degree. If we look at concrete examples of laws and natural examples of logically equivalent sentences, we find that Hempel is simply right about scientific practice; that there is no plausible way to get around this. If the equivalence condition fails at all, it must fail in some rather subtle way, and not in the natural cases of equivalents (such as contrapositives). The equivalence condition has a strong claim as a criterion of adequacy for any measure of the well-confirmedness of laws.

IB4. CONVERTIBLE CONFIRMATION

Criterion I, the criterion of supporting the paradigm predictive inference, rules out probability of the universal material conditional and instance confirmation as acceptable measures of the well-confirmedness of laws, although it is compatible with qualified instance confirmation. The equivalence condition, although compatible with probability of the universal material conditional and with instance confirmation, rules out qualified instance confirmation. (For, as we have seen, $Pr(Ga$ given $Fa)$ may be high, while $Pr(\sim Fa$ given $\sim Ga)$ is low.) Is it possible for *any* reasonable measure to satisfy both criterions I and II?

No, it is not. Any law, "All Fs are Gs," has a quasi-equivalent, *"Anything both an F and a non-G is both an F and a non-F,"* whose qualified instance confirmation is zero. Thus the only measure which could satisfy both I and II is the one that awards every law a well-confirmedness of zero. The nature of the case, however, means that the difficulty is not very damaging. Such odd laws are not among the natural examples of quasi-equivalents we had in mind when considering the equivalence condition. One would not expect to find such a law written in a science text. That this oddity has a logical source becomes clear when we consider the paradigm predictive function of laws. Such laws could never be used to set up a paradigm predictive argument, *since the instantiation of the antecedent constitutes a counterexample to the law*. The very information necessary to set up the paradigm predictive inference must invalidate the law on which it rests. The loss of such odd quasi-equivalents as paradigm predictive instruments is thus no real loss at all, for they are, *by virtue of their form*, logically defective for such purposes.

Let us call a law, the instantiation of whose antecedent is incompatible with the instantiation of its consequent, *Pickwickian*. It will do no violence to our intuitions regarding the paradigm predictive function of laws if we exclude Pickwickian laws from the scope of criterion I. The amended criterion then says that well-confirmedness of any non-Pickwickian law can be no greater than its qualified instance confirmation:

Criterion I'

If L is non-Pickwickian, $C(L) \leq$ Qualified Instance Confirmation (L).

Suppose now that we have a measure which satisfies both criterions I' and II. If a law is well confirmed according to such a measure, we can use it with confidence to set up a paradigm predictive argument. Furthermore, we can "convert" it to any non-Pickwickian quasi-equivalent ("alternative formulation of the same hypothesis") and use *that* law with confidence in setting up a paradigm predictive argument. Accordingly, I will call any measure which satisfies both criterions I' and II a *measure of convertible confirmation*.[14]

---

14. Notice that any law that has the virtue of a high score or some measure of convertible confirmation, must be at least as virtuous with regard to instance confirmation.

IB5. INSTANTIAL RESILIENCY IS THE MOST GENEROUS
         MEASURE OF CONVERTIBLE CONFIRMATION.

Is there a measure of convertible confirmation? In this section, we will show that with a few provisos instantial
resiliency (that is, the resiliency of the *material* conditional $Fa \supset Ga$ which instantiates the law) is a measure of
convertible confirmation and is the *most generous* measure of convertible confirmation.

   First the provisos. The equivalence condition will be
construed modestly. Let the relevant factors that generate
the a-instantial language be $F_1 \ldots F_n$. We will consider
equivalents to: $(x)(Fx \supset Gx)$ which are of the form $(x)(Hx
\supset Ix)$, where H and I are Boolean combinations of F, G, F_1
$\ldots F_n$. H and I do not themselves contain any quantifiers
or individual constants. This assures that $Ha \supset Ia$ will
occur in the a-instantial language. Resiliency will be construed strongly. The *predicates of the law*, together with
the factors $F_1 \ldots F_n$, will be allowed to generate the conditions under which the probability in question must bear
up. That is, the resiliency of $Fa \supset Ga$ will here be taken to
be the minimum of $Pr(Fa \supset Ga$ given $p_i)$, where the p_is are
sentences of the a-instantial language which are consistent with $Fa \supset Ga$. The modest construal of the equivalence condition together with the bold construal of resiliency lead immediately to the desired results.

   Confirmation Theorem I (C-I):

            The resiliency of $Fa \supset Ga$ is a measure of conver-
            tible confirmation for the law "All Fs are Gs"
            (where resiliency and the equivalence condition
            are relativized to the same list of factors).

   Proof:

            Equivalence: If F, G, H, I are free of quantifiers and
            individual constants, then if $(x)(Fx \supset Gx)$ and
            $(x)(Hx \supset Ix)$ are logically equivalent, so are $Fa \supset
            Ga$ and $Ha \supset Ia$; and thus the associated laws have
            the same instantial resiliency.
            Paradigm Predictive Function: If the law "All Fs
            are Gs" is non-Pickwickian, then by definition Fa
            is consistent with Ga. So Fa is consistent with $Fa
            \supset Ga$. Then the resiliency of $Fa \supset Ga \leqslant Pr(Fa \supset$

Ga given Fa). But $Pr(Fa \supset Ga$ given $Fa) = Pr(Ga$ given $Fa)$ QED.

Confirmation Theorem II (C-II):

    If M is a measure of convertible confirmation, then M(All Fs are Gs) $\leqslant$ Resiliency $(Fa \supset Ga)$.

Proof:

    Suppose the contrary, M(All Fs are Gs), is greater than $Pr(Fa \supset Ga$ given $Ha)$ for some proposition Ha of the a-instantial language compatible with $Fa \supset Ga$. But then $(x)(Fx \supset Gx)$ has as a logical equivalent, $(x)\{[(Ha \lor (Fx \,\&\, \sim Gx)] \supset [Ha \,\&\, (Fx \supset Gx)]\}$. If M obeys the equivalence condition, the law to which this corresponds must have the same M-value. Furthermore, it must be non-Pickwickian, since Ha is compatible with $Fa \supset Ga$. The qualified instance confirmation of this law is $Pr[Ha \,\&\, (Fa \supset Ga)$ given $Ha \lor (Fa \,\&\, \sim Ga)]$, which by elementary probability theory must be less than or equal to $Pr(Fa \supset Ga$ given $Ha)$. But then the M-value of the non-Pickwickian law would be greater than its qualified instance confirmation, violating criterion I'.

Let us say that one measure of confirmation is at least as *generous* as another if and only if the first assigns at least as high a value to every law under every probability distribution. C-II shows that instantial resiliency over the language is maximal for convertible confirmation in just this sense. Furthermore, it is clear that there cannot be two distinct maximal measures, for if they are distinct they must disagree on the value of some law under some distribution and they cannot both be maximal with respect to that value. Instantial resiliency is the most generous measure of convertible confirmation.

Since resiliency is relativized to a list of factors, so is convertible confirmation. Since there is no absolute resiliency,[15] there is no absolute convertible confirmation. If we proceed to additional factors over which instantial resiliency breaks down, then either the paradigm predictive

15. Especially given the strong way in which resiliency is taken for *C-I* and *C-II*.

argument or the equivalence condition[16] must be sac-
rificed. Should this conclusion seem unpleasant, please
note well that it is not due to any particular doctrine about
laws that *I* am advocating. It is simply a fact of life.

IB6. NOMIC FORCE

In "What Is a Law of Nature," A. J. Ayer suggested that
lawlikeness be explicated as a kind of probabilistic invariance, in a way closely connected with the concept of resiliency:

> There are many philosophers who are content to
> leave the matter there. They explain the "necessity" of
> natural laws as consisting in the fact that they hold for
> all possible, as well as actual, instances, and they dis-
> tinguish generalizations of law from generalizations of
> fact by bringing out the differences in their entailment
> of subjunctive conditionals. But while this is correct
> so far as it goes, I doubt if it goes far enough. Neither
> the notion of possible, as opposed to actual, instances
> nor that of the subjunctive conditional is so pellucid
> that these references to them can be regarded as bring-
> ing all our difficulties to an end. It will be well to try to
> take our analysis a little further if we can.
>   The theory which I am going to sketch will not
> avoid all talk of dispositions; but it will confine it to
> people's attitudes. My suggestion is that the difference
> between our two types of generalization lies not so
> much on the side of the facts which make them true or
> false, as in the attitude of those who put them forward.
> The factual information which is expressed by a
> statement of the form "for all x, if x has ϕ then x has
> ψ," is the same whichever way it is interpreted. For if
> the two interpretations differ only with respect to the
> possible, as opposed to the actual values of x, they do
> not differ with respect to anything that actually hap-
> pens. Now I do not wish to say that a difference in re-
> gard to mere possibilities is not a genuine difference,
> or that it is to be equated with a difference in the at-

16. Even in the weak version we have used for *C-I* and *C-II.*

titude of those who do the interpreting. But I do think that it can best be elucidated by referring to such differences of attitude. In short I propose to explain the distinction between generalizations of law and generalizations of fact, and thereby to give some account of what a law of nature is, by the indirect method of analyzing the distinction between treating a generalization as a statement of law and treating it as a statement of fact.

If someone accepts a statement of the form $(x)\phi x \supset \psi x$ as a true generalization of fact, he will not in fact believe that anything which has the property ϕ has any other property that leads to its not having ψ. For since he believes that everything that has ϕ has ψ, he must believe that whatever other properties a given value of x may have, they are not such as to prevent its having ψ. It may be even that he knows this to be so. But now let us suppose that he believes such a generalization to be true, without knowing it for certain. In that case there will be various properties X, X_1 . . . such that if he were to learn, with respect to any value of α of x, that α had one or more of these properties as well as ϕ, it would destroy, or seriously weaken his belief that α had ψ. Thus I believe that all the cigarettes in my case are made of Virginia tobacco, but this belief would be destroyed if I were informed that I had absent mindedly just filled my case from a box in which I keep only Turkish cigarettes. On the other hand, if I took it to be a law of nature that all the cigarettes in this case were made of Virginian tobacco, say on the ground that the case had some curious physical property which had the effect of changing any other tobacco that was put into it into Virginian, then my belief would not be weakened in this way.

Now if our laws of nature were causally independent of each other, and if, as Mill thought, the propositions which expressed them were always put forward as being unconditionally true, the analysis could proceed quite simply. We could then say that a person A was treating a statement of the form "for all x, if ϕx then ψx" as expressing a law of nature, if and only if there was no property X which was such that the information that a value α of x had X as well as ϕ would weaken his belief that α had ψ. And here we should have to admit the proviso that X did not logically entail not-ψ, and also, I suppose, that its presence was not regarded as a manifestation of not-ψ: for we do not wish to make it incompatible with treating a statement as the expression of a law that one should acknowledge a negative instance if it arises.[17]

Following Ayer, consider Goodman's famous example: "All coins in my pocket on V.E. day 1947 are silver." Suppose that it has been confirmed by looking into the pocket and finding only dimes, quarters, and half-dollars. Then we would regard the *law* as ill confirmed and the associated extensional generalization as highly probable. What is the probability of "a is a coin in Goodman's pocket on V.E. day 1945 $\supset$ a is (then) silver," given (1) a is a penny shined with mercury, or (2) a came from a pot containing mostly steel pennies, or (3) a was slyly slipped into Goodman's pocket after he had examined its contents, or simply (4) Goodman missed a when surveying the contents of his pocket. It seems clear that in each case the probability of the material conditional is degraded by conditionalization on the stated condition.

But if we ask the same questions, imagining that we are in the kind of transmutation case Ayer envisages with his box that converts all tobacco to Virginia, the generalization *is* regarded as a law; the material conditional bears up quite well under assumptions (1) through (4) and even nastier ones. Ayer goes on to modify the analysis to account for the influence of other background laws, which I shall treat a bit differently when I introduce a notion of convertible confirmation for *networks* of laws. Another modification is required for implicit boundary conditions. But these problems aside, and also putting aside the difficult question of how to explicate "a manifestation of not-ψ," Ayer's account in probabilistic terms comes to this: a single generalization, "All Fs are Gs," is well confirmed *qua* law if $Pr(Ga$ given Fa & $Ha)$ is for every H such that Ha is compatible with Ga (and also Fa, or the

conditional probability would not be defined). We might
then define a measure of confirmation qua law, *Ayer-lawlikeness*, which takes as its value the minimum of these
conditional probabilities. Ayer-lawlikeness can be
thought of as resiliency of $Pr(Ga$ given $Fa) = 1$. Along the
lines of the last section we can show that the most generous measure that guarantees Ayer-lawlikeness and
satisfies the equivalence condition is instantial resiliency.

Several writers have been struck by the fact that most
examples of "accidentally true" generalizations are
generalizations with a finite number of instances, of
whose truth we are convinced by what we take to be a
complete survey of those instances. Thus Goodman, in his
1947 article on counterfactuals, writes:

> Is there some way of so distinguishing laws from
> non-laws, among true universal statements of the kind
> in question, that laws will be the principles that will
> sustain counterfactual conditionals?
>
> Any attempt to draw the distinction by reference to
> a notion of causative force can be dismissed at once as
> unscientific. And it is clear that no purely syntactical
> criterion can be adequate, for even the most special
> descriptions of particular facts can be cast in a form
> having any desired degree of syntactical universality.
> "Book B is small" becomes "Everything that is Q is
> small" if "Q" stands for some predicate that applies
> uniquely to B. What then does distinguish a law like
>
> All butter melts at 150° F.
>
> from a true and general non-law like
>
> All the coins in my pocket are silver?
>
> Primarily, I would like to suggest, the fact that the first
> is accepted as true while many cases of it remain to be
> determined, the further, unexamined cases being pre-
> dicted to conform with it. The second sentence, on the
> contrary, is accepted as a description of contingent
> fact *after* the determination of all cases, no prediction
> of any of its instances being based upon it.[18]

18. In *Fact, Fiction and Forecast* 2d ed. (New York: Bobbs-Merrill,
1965).

In *The Structure of Science*, Nagel follows Goodman:

> In calling a statement a law, we are apparently as-
> serting at least tacitly that as far as we know the exam-
> ined instances of the statement do not form the
> exhaustive class of its instances. Accordingly, for an
> unrestricted universal to be called a law it is a plaus-
> ible requirement that the evidence for it is not known
> to coincide with its scope of predication and that,
> moreover, its scope is not known to be closed to any
> further augmentation.
>
> The rationale for this requirement is again to be
> found in the inferential uses to which statements
> called laws are normally put. The primary function of
> such statements is to explain and to predict. But if a
> statement asserts in effect no more than what is as-
> serted by the evidence for it, we are being slightly ab-
> surd when we employ the statement for explaining or
> predicting anything included in this evidence, and we
> are being inconsistent when we use it for explaining or
> predicting anything not included in that evidence. To
> call a statement a law is therefore to say more than that
> it is a presumably true unrestricted universal. To call a
> statement a law is to assign a certain function to it, and
> thereby to say in effect that the evidence on which it is
> based is assumed not to constitute the total scope of its
> predication.[19]

These observations can be assimilated to the resiliency
account if we are prepared to construe resiliency broadly.
Suppose I think it quite likely that the only things which
exhibit F are b, c, and d and furthermore that each of these
things has G. Then I will hold $Fa \supset Ga$ highly probable
since I will think it highly probable that $a = b \lor a = c \lor a =
d \lor \sim Fa$. But now consider the resiliency of $Fa \supset Ga$ over
a set of sentences that permits the expression of the
hypothesis that a *is something else*, i.e., $\sim (a = b) \& \sim (a
= c) \& \sim (a = d)$. The probability of this hypothesis may
be quite small, but presumably it is not zero. The resiliency of $Fa \supset Ga$ over this set can now be no greater than

19. P. 63.

the conditional probability $Pr[Ga$ given Fa & $\sim (a = b)$ & $\sim (a = c)$ & $\sim (a = d)]$. If now my *only* evidence for the generalization consists in my having examined b, c, and d and found that they exhibit G, it will fail to make this conditional probability high. If, on the other hand, the sort of evidence at hand is the kind that supports predictions for new instances, then it will render this conditional probability high, that is, *within* the small probability that a is something other than what I have surveyed and yet an F, a large proportion of the probability will go the case where a is also a G.

The argument so far could have been made just as well for Ayer-lawlikeness. But the generalization "All non-silver things are non–coin-in-Goodman's-pocket-on-V.E.-day" is as accidental as its contrapositive, and for the same reasons.

The resiliency analysis shows why a generalization "about" a finite class should fail the test of instantial resiliency when based solely on what is taken to be an exhaustive survey of its instances. But it gives us no reason to believe that this is the *only* place where resiliency can break down. Thus it leaves open the possibility that we may encounter other species of "accident." This is fortunate, for consider Hempel's example: "All bodies of pure gold have a mass of less than 100,000 kilograms." This is a troublesome example. Under no reasonable construal of *instance* could we believe that we had made an exhaustive survey of this generalization's instances. Nevertheless, there is some sense in which we have reasonable confidence in the generalization and can even use it for prediction. The reasonable confidence may then be thought of just as confidence in its predictive force. But predictive force may be high while resiliency is low. For instance, I would expect the probability that a is not pure gold, *given* that a has mass greater than 100,000 kilos and that a is either pure gold or pure platinum, to be unimpressive. From the other side, I expect the probability that a has a mass of less than 100,000 kilos, *given* that a is a moon of Jupiter and a is pure gold, to be small. We have to go to some lengths to break down the resiliency of Hempel's example (although I have probably not thought of the optimum properties to do it), so I would say that it has more nomic force than the generalization about coins in Goodman's pocket on V.E. day, but less than anything we would regard as a genuine law.

Another pragmatic characterization of nomic force that is widely accepted is that the more nomic force, the more central the law is to our conceptual scheme, that we are less willing to give up a law than an accidental generalization, that giving up a law is more disruptive to our conceptual scheme than giving up an accidental generalization, and the more nomic force the greater the disruption. Thus Nagel writes:

> Suppose now that, while some of the evidence for L is direct, there is also considerable indirect evidence for L (in either sense of "indirect"). But suppose also that some apparent exceptions to L are encountered. We may nevertheless be most reluctant to abandon L despite these exceptions, and for at least two reasons. In the first place, the combined direct and indirect confirmatory evidence for L may outweigh the apparently negative evidence. In the second place, in virtue of its relations to other laws and to the evidence for these latter, L does not stand alone, but its fate affects the fate of the system of laws to which L belongs. In consequence, the rejection of L would require a serious reorganization of certain parts of our knowledge. However, such a reorganization may not be feasible because no suitable replacement is momentarily available for the hitherto adequate system; and a reorganization may perhaps be avoided by reinterpreting the apparent exceptions to L, so that these latter are construed as not "genuine" exceptions after all. In that event, both L and the system to which it belongs can be "saved," despite the ostensible negative evidence for the law. This point is illustrated when an apparent failure of a law is construed as the result of careless observation or of inexpertness in conducting an experiment. But it can be illustrated by more impressive examples. Thus, the law (or principle) of the conservation of energy was seriously challenged by experiments on beta-ray decay whose outcome could not be

denied. Nevertheless, the law was not abandoned, and the existence of a new kind of entity (called a "neutrino") was assumed in order to bring the law into concordance with experimental data. The rationale for this assumption is that the rejection of the conservation law would deprive a large part of our physical knowledge of its systematic coherence. On the other hand, the law (or principle) of the conservation of parity in quantum mechanics (which asserts that, for example, in certain types of interactions atomic nuclei oriented in one direction emit beta-particles with the same intensity as do nuclei oriented in the opposite direction) has recently been rejected, even though at first only relatively few experiments indicated that the law did not hold in general. This marked difference in the fates of the energy and parity laws is an index of the different positions these assumptions occupy at a given time in the system of physical knowledge, and of the greater intellectual havoc that would ensue at that stage from abandoning the former assumption than is involved in rejecting the latter.[20]

Again, the resiliency account of nomic force meshes nicely with the pragmatic factors identified by philosophers of science. Part of the story of how the fate of L affects the fate of the system of laws to which L belongs requires a treatment of *networks* of laws, and it must be postponed until the section by that name (IB8). But the idea that the probability of laws bears up under all sorts of evidence that would crush the probability of an accidental generalization hardly needs translation into the language of resiliency.

IB7. HEMPEL'S PARADOX

A great deal has been written about Hempel's paradox of the ravens, much of it illuminating. I believe, however, that the foregoing account of laws can cast a bit more light on the paradox.

Two prima facie plausible principles, the equivalence

20. *Structure of Science*, pp. 65–66.

condition and the Nicod criterion taken as a sufficient condition (i.e., Fa & Ga confirms "All Fs are Gs"), lead to the conclusion that "All Fs are Gs" is confirmed by $\sim Fa$ & $\sim Ga$: "All ravens are black" is confirmed by observing a white glove. Most people find this conclusion paradoxical. Why does it seem so absurd? Is the absurdity a genuine *reductio* of the plausible principles or a manifestation of a psychologically seductive fallacy?

These questions need not have a single answer. The feelings of absurdity may have different origins in different people or multiple causes in a single person. In fact, I think that the main lines of analysis contained in the literature are *all correct*. Without rehearsing them, let me point out what convertible confirmation adds to the analysis of the situation.

Consider first the situation in which an observer confronts nature innocent of any background evidence whatsoever (if we may be permitted this highly artificial thought-experiment). Suppose now that he observes a very long, uninterrupted string of nonblack non-ravens. Suppose, further, that such observations might lead him to the following sort of probability distribution regarding a "new" individual, a:

$Pr(a$ is a black raven$) = \epsilon$
$Pr(a$ is a non-black raven$) = \epsilon$
$Pr(a$ is a black non-raven$) = \epsilon$
$Pr(a$ is a non-black non-raven$) = 1 - 3\epsilon$
(where ϵ is small)

Thus, although the law has high instance confirmation, it fails to have high convertible confirmation since the conditional probability that a is a raven given that it is black (among others) is an unimpressive .5. We are here faced with a failure of the paradigm predictive argument, which would not have arisen had we observed an uninterrupted string of black ravens. Here is at least one objective foundation for the feeling of absurdity.

Must we then say that Nicod was right in holding only black ravens to be confirming, and Hempel wrong in holding non-ravens as well to be confirming? *Not at all!* That inference would only be justified if we accepted the following principle connecting the concepts of confirming instance and well-confirmedness.

Principle of Well-Confirmedness (W.C.):

If E_n is evidence consisting solely of n *confirming instances* for a hypothesis, H, then there is some n such that H is *well confirmed* on E_n.

W.C. has some initial plausibility. Enough confirming instances, in the absence of any disconfirmers, should confirm a hypothesis as highly as you please. But W.C. simply does not hold for convertible confirmation. If we limit ourselves to instantial evidence, then what is required for well-confirmedness in the sense of high convertible confirmation is not simply *quantity* of confirming instances but also *variety* of confirming instances. With this proviso, we can agree with Hempel as to which instances are confirming.

But although the foregoing analysis in terms of convertible confirmation does throw some light on the odd aspects of non-black non-ravens as confirmers while preserving the equivalence condition, it fails to explain the asymmetry between black ravens and non-black non-ravens. How, then, are we to accommodate the plausible intuitions expressed by Quine in the following passage from "Natural Kinds"?

> Now I propose assimilating Hempel's puzzle to Goodman's by inferring from Hempel's that the complement of a projectible predicate need not be projectible. "Raven" and "black" are projectible; a black raven does count toward "All ravens are black." Hence a black raven counts also, indirectly, toward "All non-black things are non-ravens," since this says the same thing. But a green leaf does not count toward "All non-black things are non-ravens," nor, therefore, toward "All ravens are black"; "non-black" and "non-raven" are not projectible. "Green" and "leaf" are projectible, and the green leaf counts toward "All leaves are green" and "All green things are leaves"; but only a black raven can confirm "All ravens are black," the complements not being projectible.[21]

If we agree with Quine that a black raven confirms both

---

21. In *Ontological Relativity and Other Essays* (New York: Columbia University Press, 1969), pp. 115–16.

"All ravens are black" and its contrapositive, while a
non-black non-raven confirms neither, then, on the face of
it, neither qualified instance confirmation nor convertible
confirmation provides an explanation. But Quine also
suggests an answer. In my examples so far, I have
assumed that an observer innocent of any background
information would treat all of the four categories black
raven, non-black raven, black non-raven, non-black non-
raven on a par, with a long string of observations within a
category pumping up the probability that the next observed instance would be in that category and diminishing equally the probability that it would be in either of the
other categories. Quine suggests that we are never this innocent, even at birth. Inductive propensities to treat non-
blackness differently from blackness may very well be
wired into the human nervous system, or, if not, they may
be learned at such a deep level as to make it impossible to
imagine them away.

Perhaps it will be useful, then, to move from the highly
artificial tabula rasa model to a model of a situation that
involves quite explicit background knowledge.[22] I would
like to focus on a situation where it is quite clear (clearer
than in the case of the ravens) that Fa & Ga confirms "All
Fs are Gs" and its logical equivalents, and that $\sim Fa$ & $\sim Ga$
does not. Consider the familiar example of the determination of melting point. Let Fx say that x is a pure sample of
iron and Gx say that x melts at 1,525 degrees centigrade.
We have as a consequence of a background theory the law
that all samples of a pure metal melt at the same temperature. Here, one instance of iron melting at 1,525 C. (Fa &
Ga) is quite enough to render the law well confirmed.
Neither would we shrink from affirming, on this basis,
that all samples with a different melting point are not pure
iron. But any number of samples of substances other than
pure iron melting at whatever temperature you please
($\sim Fa$ & Ga, $\sim Fa$ & $\sim Ga$) leave the law unenhanced.

This striking asymmetry is quite in accord with the
identification of well-confirmedness of laws with convert-

22. The use of this sort of example to illuminate such situations was
suggested to me by Ralph Kennedy.

ible confirmation and, in particular, with instantial resiliency. Let a be the sample I am about to look at, and b be a further unexamined sample. I have not yet determined the melting point of iron, but I do have as well-confirmed background knowledge that all samples of pure iron will melt at the same temperature. Consider my joint probability distribution for Fa, Ga, Fb, Gb. Since my background knowledge is well confirmed, $\sim[(Fa \& Ga \& Fb \& \sim Gb) \text{ v} (Fa \& \sim Ga \& Fb \& Gb)]$ (i.e., that I will not have two samples of iron with different melting points) is *resilient. It is then a matter of algebra that conditionalizing on* Fa & Ga *carries me to a space within which* Fb ⊃ Gb *is resilient!* That is, $Fa \& Ga$ renders "All Fs are Gs" well confirmed as required. On the other hand, conditionalization of $\sim Fa \&$ $\sim Ga$ or $\sim Fa \& Ga$ has no such effect, since conditionalizing on either of these takes one into a space where the background knowledge has little effect (see figure 1).

The case of the ravens is somewhat intermediate between the two discussed so far. It has been repeatedly pointed out in the literature that we are in possession of background knowledge which is quite difficult to suppress, that is, the knowledge that there are enormous numbers of non-ravens, of all colors, in the world. Usually this is made on the basis of an argument to the effect that observation of a black raven will raise the probability of $(x) (Rx \supset Bx)$ more than observation of a non-raven. But there is also an argument to be made with respect to instantial resiliency. Suppose you are the first ornithologist to study ravens and that you possess this background knowledge. Then your probabilities with respect to the blackness and ravenhood of an unexamined individual might plausibly look something like this:

$Pr(a \text{ is a black raven}) = \epsilon$

$Pr(a \text{ is a non-black raven}) = 9\epsilon$

$Pr(a \text{ is a black non-raven}) = .1$

$Pr(a \text{ is a non-black non-raven}) = .9 - 10\epsilon$

Here observation of a long string of black ravens would plausibly move you to a space where $Ra \supset Ba$ is resilient, whereas observation of non-ravens would not. This holds, a fortiori, if we take Quine's suggestion about nonprojectibility of complements in the following sense: $Pr(Ra \&$

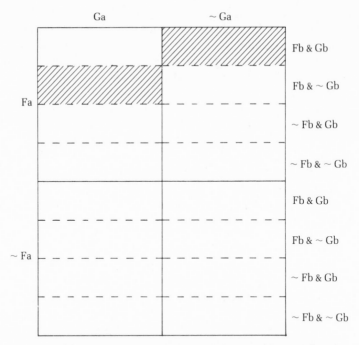

Figure 1. As a consequence of the background theory, the probability in the shaded cells is small relative to the probability of
each other cell. Conditionalizing on Fa & Ga takes us into the
upper left quadrant, within which Fb ⊃ Gb is resilient. Conditionalizing on ~ Fa & Ga or on ~ Fa & ~ Ga or on ~ Fa need
have no such effect.

Ba) is far more sensitive to observation of a string of black
ravens than Pr(~ Ba & ~ Ra) is to observation of a string
of non-black non-ravens, or Pr(Ba & ~ Ra) to observation
of a string of black non-ravens.

IB8. NETWORKS OF LAWS

Laws do not typically stand in isolation. Rather, they operate as part of a network, or theory, containing other
laws, and perhaps auxiliary statements which are not laws
as well. It may be that in the final analysis all our beliefs
should be thought of as making up one big network. It is
this view which has been so persuasively advocated by
Quine:

> The totality of our so-called knowledge or beliefs,
> from the most casual matters of geography or history
> to the profoundest laws of atomic physics or even of
> pure mathematics and logic, is a man-made fabric
> which impinges on experience only along the edges.
> Or, to change the figure, total science is like a field of
> force, those boundary conditions are experience. A
> conflict with experience at the periphery occasions
> readjustments in the interior of the field. Truth values
> have to be redistributed over some of our state-
> ments. . . . No particular experiences are linked with
> any particular statements in the interior of the field,
> except indirectly through considerations of equilib-
> rium affecting the field as a whole.[23]

Without rushing to global considerations, I would like
to ask the modest question: How is the confirmation of a
finite network of laws to be evaluated? The most obvious
way in which laws are interconnected in a network is that
one law functions under the assumption that the other
laws in the network are correct. Consequently, in evaluating a law within a network we are interested in how its
probability bears up under all conditions which *do not
violate any member of the network*. The preceding discussion of instantial resiliency suggests a simple
generalization to networks. For a network of laws, "All F_1s
are G_1s," . . . "All F_ns are G_ns," take its confirmation as the
resiliency of the conjunction of its instances: $R[(F_1a \supset G_1a)$
& $(F_2a \supset G_2a)$ & . . . $(F_na \supset G_na)]$. This measure of convertible confirmation satisfies an *equivalence condition*. If
one network is gotten from another by substitution of
quasi-equivalent laws, then their degree of confirmation
must be the same.[24]

It also satisfies a kind of *consequence condition*. This
is all the more interesting because resiliency *per se* does
not satisfy a straightforward consequence condition. A
law may have higher resiliency than one of its quasi-

23. "Two Dogmas of Empiricism," in *From a Logical Point of View*,
2d ed. (Cambridge: Harvard University Press, 1961), p. 42.
24. Under the same assumptions about the character of the Fs which
were invoked in the section on resiliency and convertible confirmation.

consequences. But what we can do is *add* a quasi-consequence of a network of laws to the network to form an enlarged network which suffers no diminution in instantial resiliency.

Network Theorem I:

>Let N be a network of laws, C be defined as the resiliency over the language of the conjunction of the instantiations of the laws with respect to a, L be a quasi-consequence of N, and N_L be the network formed by adding L to N. Then:
>
>$$C(N_L) = C(N)$$

Proof:

>If L is a quasi-consequence of N, then, by definition, L's associated universal material conditional is a consequence of those associated with the members of N. Then the instantiation of L must be a consequence of the instantiations of the members of N. But then the conjunction of the instantiations of N_L is logically equivalent to the conjunction of the instantiations of N, and must therefore have equal resiliency.

What can we say about how networks fulfill the paradigm predictive function of laws? To state the connection we must introduce the concept of being *Pickwickian with respect to a network*. A law is Pickwickian with respect to a network just in case the joint instantiation of its antecedent and its consequent is incompatible with the conjunction of (the extensional counterparts of) the laws in the network. For example, "Every closed system whose total energy increases through time has nondecreasing entropy through time" is not Pickwickian *simpliciter* but is Pickwickian in the context of a network which includes the law of conservation of energy. Now it is clear from Network Theorem I that a well-confirmed network may contain such odd laws, the example just cited being a quasi-consequence of the second law of phenomenological thermodynamics. What we might reasonably expect, then, and what is in fact the case, is that well-confirmedness of the network should guarantee high qualified instance confirmation (QIC) for all its members which are not Pickwickian with respect to the network.

Network Theorem II:

> Let N be a network of laws and L be a member of N
> which is not Pickwickian with respect to N. Then:
> $$QIC(L) \geq C(N)$$

Proof:

> Let $INST$ be the conjunction of instantiations of
> members of N with respect to a. Let L be "All Fs
> are Gs." Since L is not Pickwickian with respect to
> the network, Fa is compatible with $INST$. Then,
> since we are taking $C(N)$ to be $R(INST)$, by the resi-
> liency theorem, $Pr(INST$ given $Fa) \geq C(N)$. But, by
> algebra, $PR(Ga$ given $Fa) \geq Pr(INST$ given $Fa)$.

Networks exhibit a heirarchical organization which
reveals itself in the confirmation values of their subnetworks. If the confirmation of a subnetwork is at least as
high as the confirmation of the network, then the predictive force of the subnetwork will survive intact upon the
discovery of instances which falsify other members of the
network. For this reason I will call N' a *stable core of* N iff
(1) all the members of N' are in N and (2) $C(N') \geq$
$C(N)$("being a stable core of" is a partial order relation").

The notion of a network can be extended to include
other statements of the language as well as laws. For
example, we might have an extended network containing
the statements: All Fs are Gs, All Hs are Is, and Fb & $\sim Ib$. I
will take the confirmation of such an extended network to
be the resiliency of the conjunction of the instantiations of
the laws with the other sentences involved; in the exam-
ple $R[(Fa \supset Ga)$ & $(Ha \supset Ia)$ & $(Fb$ & $\sim Ib)]$. It is reasonable
to extend the notion of a network in this way because it is
reasonable for statements other than instances of laws to
achieve some substantial degree of resiliency. Good clear
current observation can, and ought to, produce a belief
state in which statements describing that belief state are
widely resilient. G. E. Moore's "I now see a hand before
me" and other similar statements are cases in point. Of
course, it may be too strong to have resiliency over an entire language with rich descriptive machinery, *which is
exactly what the standard skeptical arguments point out*
(i.e., they point out that there is a supposition consistent
with the statement in question—evil demon, hypnosis,

hologram, mirrors, etc.—under which the probability of that statement breaks down).

We are now in a position to move a little closer toward Quine's picture of knowledge. Our knowledge comprises one big network, and its internal structure can be mapped by looking at the confirmation relations between its various subnetworks. Without pursuing the matter further at this point, I offer two small examples:

1. Consider a highly confirmed network consisting of the law of conservation of energy, L_1, and the second law of thermodynamics, L_2. Assume a structure of confirmation such that if you discovered a counterinstance to L_1 you would lose a great deal of confidence in the instances of L_2, but if you discovered a counterinstance of L_2 you would retain your confidence in instances of L_1. Then L_1 is a *stable core* of the network (L_1, L_2), while L_2 is not.

2. (a) Suppose we have purely intensional evidence for the proposition that either Moriarty is in London, L, or in Singapore, S. Then $C(L \vee S)$ may be high, but $C(L \vee S, L)$; $C(L \vee S, S)$; $C(L \vee S, L, S)$ are not. (b) Suppose we have strong evidence that Moriarty is in London and believe that he is in London or Singapore solely on that basis. Then $C(L, L \vee S)$ may be high and L may be a *stable core* of $(L, L \vee S)$ while $L \vee S$ is not. (c) Suppose we have strong evidence that Moriarty is in London, but independently have strong intensional evidence that he is either in London or Singapore. Then $C(L, L \vee S)$ may be high, and both L and $L \vee S$ may be stable cores of that network.

IB9. EPISTEMIC AND OBJECTIVE RESILIENCY AND THE CON-
     FIRMATION OF UNIVERSAL LAWS

The considerations brought forward in chapter IB all appear to argue for the high *epistemic* resiliency of $Fa \supset Ga$ as a criterion of confirmation of the law "All Fs are Gs." How does this square with the idea that a universal law may be thought of as asserting that everything within the scope of its quantifier has a propensity of one not to be a counterexample, taken together with the account of propensities given in chapter IA?

In chapter IA, propensities were construed as resilient *objective* probabilities. The resiliency requirement is for the *objective* probability distribution, not the epistemic one. A propensity statement is *well confirmed* if the epistemic probability is high that the correct objective distribution gives the probability attribution at issue high resiliency. In other words, confirmation of propensity statements goes by *epistemic expectation of objective resiliency.*

If the account of propensities in chapter IA is correct, and if the instantial-propensity-not-to-be-a-counterexample interpretation of universal laws is correct, then a well-confirmed law, "All Fs are Gs," should have a high *epistemic* expectation of the objective resiliency of $Fa \supset Ga$. (Remember that "Resiliency of $Fa \supset Ga$" in the terminology of this section is short for "Resiliency of $Pr(Fa \supset Ga) = 1$" in the terminology of chapter IA.) This requirement is not quite the same as the requirement of high epistemic resiliency, although we may have to go to some lengths to find an example where they diverge. It is worth looking for such an example, since, by the results of section IB5, convertible confirmation is tied to *epistemic* resiliency. If we find an example of a well-confirmed law where instantial resiliency fails, then either the equivalence condition or the paradigm predictive function of laws must fail there as well.

Suppose that the law "All sodium salts burn yellow" is well confirmed: you are handed an unknown substance and put it into the flame; it clearly burns green. You therefore decide that it is probably not sodium. But your faith in your eyes is more unshakable than your faith in the empirical law; if you were convinced that it was sodium, you would reject the law. But, as you were not so convinced, the law is still well confirmed. Then the *epistemic* conditional probability that this sample burns yellow given that it is sodium is low. So the instantial resiliency and paradigm predictive function of a well-confirmed law break down with respect to this instance.

This result is not really embarrassing for scientific

methodology. The fact that we have observed it with respect to the consequent of the law but not the antecedent renders it nonexchangeable; the fact that this sample burned green, not yellow, implies that if we were to learn that the sample was sodium we would hardly want to apply the law to it for prediction. The law in this example retains its predictive force for unexamined samples. Still, we would like our theory of the confirmation of laws to give an account of this example.

The theory that a universal law asserts that each instance has a high propensity to accord with that law allows us to give such an account. Consider two objective distributions corresponding to the sample being sodium, pr_s; to it not being sodium, $pr_{\sim s}$. After our observation that the sample burned green, the instantial resiliency of the law in pr_s is destroyed, but its instantial resiliency in $pr_{\sim s}$ is unaffected. Furthermore, the epistemic probability of $pr_{\sim s}$ is high and that of pr_s low; we think that it is unlikely that the sample *is* sodium because it burned green. The *epistemic expectation of objective resiliency* is still high, and the law is well confirmed. Of course, if we were now to be convinced by other tests that the sample was indeed a sodium salt, our epistemic probability would shift from $pr_{\sim s}$ to pr_s and the law would be disconfirmed.

The resiliency requirement for the confirmation of laws is thus best seen as a requirement of objective resiliency. A well-confirmed law has a high epistemic expectation of objective resiliency. The application of laws via the equivalence condition and paradigm predictive argument is explained by the fact that a high expectation of objective resiliency typically carries with it a not inconsiderable amount of epistemic resiliency. The scope of epistemic resiliency may be smaller. A well-confirmed law will not be epistemically resilient over descriptions of possible evidence that would tend to disconfirm it. So a well-confirmed law will, quite properly, refrain from predicting that if it is disconfirmed it will still hold.

IC Generalizations

IC1*. RESILIENCY IN INFINITE PROBABILITY SPACES

So far we have only dealt with resiliency in finite probability spaces. From an ultrapragmatic standpoint, this is as far as we need or ought to go. The area of the universe that need ever really concern us must have some finite bounds, whether or not the universe itself is finite. Likewise, whatever phase space we consider relevant can be chopped up into tiny cells. Thus for this finitized picture of the world the number of possible scientific hypotheses is also finite, and so forth. So the ultrapragmatic story goes.

I believe that there is a great deal to be learned by looking at science from the ultrapragmatic standpoint, but that ultimately it fails to give a correct picture of the idealizing aspect of science. Even though our measurements are only accurate to a certain number of decimal places, we frame our hypotheses in terms of continuous magnitudes, and science would be conceptually devastated if we could not do so. Idealization buys conceptual simplification. In another sense of pragmatism, the importation of the infinite into science via continuous magnitudes is pragmatically justified: "By their fruits!" The pragmatic status of the infinitely large in science is more clouded, but continuity alone is more than enough to force us to consider spaces of possibilities which are infinite.

However, this fattening of our space of possibilities *appears to be incompatible* with strict coherence (regularity). When the possibility space is even denumerable, it is impossible to give each possibility an equal non-zero probability. For nonuniform distributions on a denumerable possibility space it is possible to give each possibility finite probability in certain ways (e.g., $Pr(1) = 1/2, Pr(2) = 1/4, \ldots Pr(N) = 1/2N$), but even this possibility vanishes when we move to nondenumerable spaces. There we have no option but to assign zero probability to some possibilities, and consequently a probability of one to some proposition (= set of possibilities) which may possibly be false. *Strict coherence fails*; if we interpret probability as a fair betting quotient there is a bet which we will consider fair even though we can possibly lose it but cannot possibly win it.

The problems that irregularity generates are not confined to the static problem of applying a probability distribution. They also include complications of the dynamics. How can a proposition of prior probability zero come to have a posterior probability different from zero? How do we assimilate new knowledge of a proposition with a prior probability of zero? It seems that if we want to avoid dogmatic, unrevisable judgments being forced on us *by the mathematics of the probability representation*, we must devise special external rules of belief-change for propositions with zero prior probability. This can be done. And perhaps at any rate we will need external rules for some cases of belief-change not properly treated by conditionalization. But the choice should be dictated by epistemological considerations, not by the mathematics of the probability representation.

What has gone wrong? Mathematically, the answer is quite clear. We have fattened the *domain* of the probability function (the space of possibilities) without any concomitant fattening of its *range* (the numerical probability values). The reals between zero and one aren't enough. We need a richer mathematical structure within which to locate our probability values. The objection is bound to be raised that such a richer mathematical structure is hardly realistic for probabilities which are supposed, in some sense, to be rational *degrees of belief*. Indeed, it is not realistic; it is an idealization. And—to belabor the point—it is an idealization of the range of the probability function designed to accommodate in a smooth way an idealization in the domain of the probability function. To promote idealization at one end and resist it at the other is philosophically perverse.

What sort of mathematical structure do we need? The answer again is clear. If we want to spread our probabilities out over a rich (nondenumerable) infinite space of possibilities such that each possibility has non-zero probability, we will have to spread it somewhere infinitesimally thin. We need to fatten up the reals between zero and one with the addition of infinitesimals. How do we go about constituting such a structure?

In 1961 Abraham Robinson rescued the infinitesimal from philosophical disrepute, and set it on a firm foundation, by using a nonstandard model of the real numbers. Consider a first-order *language of analysis*. This language may be taken as very rich, to the point of having a name for every real number, an operation symbol for every operation on the reals, and a relational symbol for every relation on the reals. The set of true statements of this language is the theory of *analysis*. It has a model: the intended model on the reals. Now add to the theory of analysis the sentences $v > r_i$ for a fixed variable v and for every r_i which is a name-for-a-real. Every finite subset of this set of sentences has a model—the intended model of analysis—so, by the general compactness theorem for first-order languages, it must have a model. This model must assign the variable v an "infinite" element which, according to the extension of the greater-than relational symbol, is greater than each element assigned to a name-for-a-real. Thus this model cannot be the intended model of analysis; but it is still *a* model of analysis, a nonstandard model. We know a lot about such a model on the basis of just these two facts: first, that it contains an "infinite" element in the sense just explained, and, second, that it *is* a model of analysis—it makes every true first-order statement of analysis true. For instance, it is a true, first-order statement of analysis that every number has a reciprocal; likewise that, if x is greater than y, its reciprocal is less than that of y. Consequently, since our nonstandard model contains "infinite" elements, it must also contain their reciprocals, which must be "infinitesimal" in the same sense. The same technique can even be extended to higher-order languages of analysis, provided that the nonstandard model is allowed to be a general model in the sense of Henkin (that is to say, its higher-order quantifiers may be interpreted as ranging only over a subset of their natural domain.)

Such nonstandard models are the natural place to look for a suitable fattened range for the probability function. There is no point in playing the tailor if a perfect fit can be found on the rack. We have here the reals enriched with infinitesimals, and infinitesimals *which must be exceptionally well behaved* since they satisfy all the first-order statements of analysis.

Can we find nonstandard models which give us infinitesimals in a way which will mesh nicely with classical measure theory? This question is answered positively in the work of Bernstein and Wattenberg on nonstandard measure theory. They demonstrate the existence of a measure on the unit interval such that it is defined on *all* subsets of the unit interval, and for all Lebesgue measurable sets it differs at most by an infinitesimal from the Lebesgue measure of those sets. Furthermore, each nonempty set receives positive (possibly infinitesimal) measure and the infinitesimal measures can be compared with natural results. For instance, the measure of the rational points in (0, 1/2) is twice the measure of the rational points in (0, 1/4), whereas the Lebesgue measure of both sets is zero. We can then imagine throwing a point dart at a unit interval target and have the conditional probability of hitting a rational point within (0, 1/4), given that we hit a rational point within (0, 1/2), assume the intuitively correct value when defined in the standard Kolmogoroff way $[Pr(q$ given $p) = Pr(p \ \& \ q)/Pr(p)]$. I will reserve technical details for an appendix and proceed in this section on the assumption that my probability function has the nonstandard reals as its range in such a way that strict coherence is preserved.

Now we are ready to define a strong sense of the *resiliency* of a proposition within this enriched framework. But first one small technical detail: a nonstandard real number has a unique representation as the sum of a standard real number and infinitesimal. Thus we are entitled to refer to the *standard part* of any nonstandard real number. Now, for any proposition q:

Def: The resiliency of q = greatest lower bound of the set of all numbers, n, such that n is the standard part of $Pr(q$ given $p)$ for some p consistent with q.

(Since the set of propositions p consistent with q is now infinite, "minimum" in the old definition is now replaced by "greatest lower bound." Since not all sets of nonstandard reals are well ordered, we take our bound over the standard parts of the relevant conditional probabilities rather than over the conditional probabilities themselves. Thus $Res(q)$ is always well defined.)

We have frequently emphasized that the requirements for high resiliency become more stringent as the language becomes richer. We are now set up to handle extremely rich languages, and we may expect that high resiliency becomes accordingly more difficult to attain. Let us say that a language, together with a probability distribution on that language, is *spread-out* iff every proposition of the language with positive probability is entailed by a proposition of the language with infinitesimal probability. (This situation should not be atypical for rich languages. For instance, recall the example of the point dart and the unit interval, and let the propositions be of the form that the point that the dart hits is in S, where S is some subset of the unit interval.) Let us also say that a probability or resiliency is *almost* equal to a certain value iff it differs at most infinitesimally from that value. Then the following theorem shows how difficult high resiliency is to attain in spread-out languages.

Theorem:

If a language, together with a probability distribution on it, is *spread-out*, then for any proposition in that language its resiliency is equal to zero or its probability is almost equal to one.

Proof:

If $Pr(p)$ is not almost equal to one, $Pr(\sim p)$ is finite. Since the probabilities are spread-out, p is entailed by a proposition p^* with infinitesimal probability. Then $\sim p \vee p^*$ is a proposition consistent with p which has finite probability and $Pr(p$ given $\sim p \vee p^*)$ must be at most infinitesimal. So $Res(p)$ is almost equal to zero.

The preceding theorem not only shows that resiliency over a rich language is hard to attain; it also raises the possibility that the concept of resiliency might be trivialized in spread-out probability spaces, collapsing into that of probability almost equal to one. If this were so, it would

constitute a serious challenge to the significance of the resiliency concept in rich languages, since the property of
being spread-out can hardly be considered pathological.
But it is not so.

> *Proposition:*
>
>> It is *not* the case that probability almost equal to
>> one in a spread-out probability distribution over a
>> language is a sufficient condition for resiliency
>> almost equal to one, *or even for finite positive re-*
>> *siliency.*

> *Example:*
>
>> Returning to our example of uniform measure on
>> the unit interval, consider the proposition that the
>> dart hits an irrational number. Its probability is
>> almost equal to one. But its probability *given that*
>> it hit $1/\pi$ or $1/4$ is one-half; its probability given
>> that it hits $1/\pi$ or $1/4$ or $1/5$ is one-third, etc. So its
>> resiliency must be almost equal to zero.

IC2*. Resiliency of the Universal Generalization and Its Relation to Instantial Resiliency

I took the paradox of provisional acceptance as being a
strong argument for looking for a confirmation of laws
among instantial concepts: instance confirmation, qualified instance confirmation, and finally instantial resiliency. There are those who want to set higher standards
for laws to be well confirmed, that the universal generalization $(x)(Fx \supset Gx)$ and not only its instances should be
held in high regard. Those who are of this mind will want
to deal with the paradox of provisional acceptance in
some alternative way. I venture no suggestions as to how
that might be done, but I do appreciate the attractiveness
of those impeccable standards which require that, for a
law to be well confirmed, it must be well confirmed *qua*
generalization about all instances throughout all space-
time. For such a stronger sense of confirmation we now
have a natural candidate to consider:

> Resiliency of $(x)(Fx \supset Gx)$

with which we now have the means to deal. In this sec-

tion, I would like to compare this "generality"—
confirmation with corresponding instantial concepts.

But first I have to finish developing of the instantial
concepts. Carnap introduced not only instance confirmation $Pr(Fa \supset Ga)$ but also n-ary instance confirmation
$Pr[(Fa_1 \supset Ga_1) \& \ldots \& (Fa_n \supset Ga_n)]$. Qualified instance
confirmation does not generalize to n places so smoothly,
since a conjunction of conditional probabilities makes no
sense. (One might try $Pr(Ga_1 \& \ldots \& Ga_n$ given
$Fa_1 \& \ldots \& Fa_n).$) Convertible confirmation based on the
resiliency concept can, however, be generalized quite
smoothly to n instances as Resiliency $[(Fa_1 \supset Ga_1) \& \ldots \&
(Fa_n \supset Ga_n)]$.

It is possible to carry the development of instantial
concepts one step further, by means of limits. Take any
infinite set of individual constants (a_i) and consider the
greatest lower bound of the probabilities of conjunction of
any finite length, $Pr(Fa_j \supset Ga_j \& \ldots \& Fa_k \supset Ga_k)$, where
the constants are in that set. Call this the ω-instance
confirmation of $(x)(Fx \supset Gx)$. N-ary convertible confirmation based on instantial resiliency can be extended to
ω-convertible confirmation in an entirely analogous manner.

But if it is not certain that the individual constants in
(a_i) name just the things in the domain, or if the probability measure does not have very special limit properties,
then the ω-instance confirmation of a universal generalization may not equal its probability and its ω-convertible
confirmation may not equal its resiliency. The move to the
level of generality is a genuine leap, outstripping all the
instantial concepts, even the ω-instantial concepts. What,
then, is the relation between resiliency of the universal
generalization and instantial resiliency? Suppose we start
with a first-order language with individual constants, L,
and for any finite set of individual constants of L, $\{a_i\}$, let
L_{a_i} be the sublanguage of L which consists of quantifier-
free statements which have as their only individual constants members of $\{a_i\}$. The L_{a_i}s are suitable sublanguages
within which to evaluate instantial resiliency. Now consider a universal generalization $(x)(Fx \supset Gx)$, where F and

G are contexts free of quantifiers and individual constants. Then we can say that:

$$R_{L_{a_i}}[(Fa_i \supset Ga_i) \& \ldots \& (Fa_n \supset a_n)] \geqslant R_L(x)(Fx \supset Gx)$$

where $\{a_i\} = \{a_1, a_2, \ldots a_n\}$

For the probability of the conjunction of instances given some sentence, p, must be at least as great as the probability of the universal generalization given p. And the statements *in the sublanguage in question* which are consistent with the conjunction of instances are also consistent with the universal generalization. (Notice that the restriction is essential; e.g., consider $(\exists x)(Fx \& \sim Gx)$.) Thus, if the probability of the universal generalization given any statement of L consistent with it is high, the probability of the conjunction of instances given any statement of L_{a_i} consistent with it must be at least as high. In this sense we can say that high resiliency of the universal generalization guarantees high instantial resiliency. (It follows from the foregoing that this holds, mutatis mutandis, for ω-convertible confirmation as well.)

Bearing the foregoing qualifications in mind, and bearing in mind the fact that resiliency over the language is stronger than resiliency over a sublanguage and the relative strengths of ω, n-ary, and simple instantial concepts, the relative strengths of the various measures suggested as measures of the well-confirmedness of laws can be summarized in the following diagram:

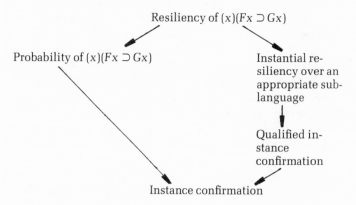

Resiliency of $(x)(Fx \supset Gx)$

Probability of $(x)(Fx \supset Gx)$

Instantial resiliency over an appropriate sublanguage

Qualified instance confirmation

Instance confirmation

THE PRAGMATICS
OF LAWS

The proof of the pudding is in the eating. The proof of a theory of the confirmation of laws is in how well it meshes with plausible accounts of the uses to which well-confirmed laws are put. One of the central uses to which well-confirmed laws are put is making predictions, and that use has already played a central role in the investigations of part I. But well-confirmed laws have other uses as well. They support both indicative and subjunctive conditionals, and indeed the support of subjunctives is often taken to be the mark of lawlikeness. Laws have some connection with singular causal statements, although the status of the latter in current discussions is problematic and almost all questions pertaining to them are in hot dispute. That the essence of scientific explanation of particular facts consists in embedding these facts in a network of scientific law is, I think, beyond serious dispute, but the nature of the embedding required is not. That lawlike or causal connections are an indispensable requirement for true perception and for a broad spectrum of cases of knowledge is an insight that goes back at least to Hume, but it is one for which we have renewed appreciation today. It is plausible that lawlike and causal connections should form a framework within which we make rational decisions. It seems almost a truism that our rational decisions should take into account our rational beliefs about which events those decisions may influence.

Taken on the whole, this is territory where theory is a beggar and counterexample is king. I am under no illusion that an unexceptionable, comprehensive theory of the pragmatics of laws is at hand. But I do believe that conditional probability and resiliency are unifying concepts that run through the entire range of these concepts, and thus illuminate their relation to the concept of law.

IIA Conditionals

If ifs and cans
were pots and pans
there'd be no need
for tinkers' hands.

Mother Goose

What might have been
is an abstraction
remaining a perpetual possibility
only in the world of speculation

T. S. Eliot
Burnt Norton

IIA1. CONVERSATIONAL IMPLICATURE, RESILIENCY AND CONDITIONALS: CAN THE INDICATIVE CONDITIONAL BE CONSTRUED AS THE MATERIAL CONDITIONAL PLUS CONVERSATIONAL IMPLICATURE?

Conditionals have been a puzzle at least since the Stoics, who debated the relative merits of their versions of material, formal, and strict implication so vigorously that "even the crows in the trees were cawing about the meanings of conditionals." The puzzle runs deep enough to survive in modern languages, and the "paradoxical" aspects of the material conditional have proved annoying enough to C. I. Lewis, Wilhelm Ackerman, and Alan Anderson and Nuel Belnap to motivate construction of variant systems of "strict implication" or "entailment."

In his William James Lectures, *Logic and Conversation,* Paul Grice presented a theory of conversational implicature which holds out new hope for the Philonian theory that the ordinary indicative conditional is the material conditional.[1] The leading idea of the theory of conversational implicature is that in normal circumstances certain rules of cooperation are in force, and are understood to be in force by both the speaker and the hearer. This tacit understanding remains in effect unless explicitly canceled and forms the framework within which information is transmitted. It is not part of the meanings of the terms involved, as is shown by the fact that it can be explicitly canceled, that is, the speaker may simply notify the hearer that he will not follow the customary cooperative rules to their fullest extent, but will nevertheless stick to literal meanings and say things that are literally true. For instance, if I have good reason to believe that Moriarty is in London, and on the sole basis of this evidence tell Holmes that Moriarty is either in London or in Singapore, I shall have violated the rules of cooperation, for Holmes will naturally assume that my evidence has some positive relevance to the possibility that Moriarty is in Singapore, which it has not. If, however, the presumption is explicitly canceled—I say, "I know where Moriarty is, but I will only give you a clue; he is either in Barcelona or in London"—then I carry on a perfectly acceptable English conversation. Certainly, no violation of the meaning of or takes place! Thus the gap between the use of or in ordinary conversation and its truth-functional meaning is bridged by implicature, and the need for the "intentional or" of Anderson and Belnap is removed. It is likewise for other sentences, and thus a whole menage of exotic connectives is eliminated in favor of one rule of conversation.[2]

1. See also H. P. Grice, "Logic and Conversation," in P. Cole and J. Morgan, eds., *Syntax and Semantics*, vol. 3 (New York: Academic Press, 1975), and the further discussions of conversational implicature in P. Cole, ed., *Syntax and Semantics Vol. 9: (Pragmatics)* (New York: Academic Press, 1978).

2. But how are we to state the rule of conversation operating in the foregoing example? To say that we must assert the most specific statement for which we have evidence would be too stringent, for that would limit us to long recitals of our evidence. Perhaps we should say that assertion of a statement normally carries the presumption that of all the compound sentences that we can construct *out of its subsentences*, it is the most specific one which is highly probable on the evidence. This

Can the indicative conditional be construed as the material conditional plus conversational implicature? I think

would explain why "Moriarty is somewhere," although unhelpful, is not misleading in the way that "Moriarty is in London or Singapore" is. This formulation can be seen to be quite closely connected with the idea a *resiliency simpliciter*, i.e., resiliency of a sentence over the set of its atomic subsentences. A more specific sentence than S (a sentence of which S is a logical consequence), S', can be asserted almost as strongly as S on the evidence if and only if $Pr(S \& \sim S')$ is small. If it is small *relative to* $Pr(\sim S)$ then $Pr[S$ given $\sim S \vee (S \& \sim S')]$ is small and so is the resiliency simpliciter of S.

To put the matter precisely, let us say that a sentence, S, is ϵ-*maximally specific* if and only if the probability of the least probable sentence, P, framed in terms of subsentences of S which entails S is ϵ. Then $pr(S) - pr(S \& \sim P) = \epsilon$, so ϵ may be thought of as the cost, in terms of absolute degradation of probability, of asserting the more specific sentence $S \& \sim P$. Then the *resiliency simpliciter* of such an ϵ-maximally specific sentence, S, is equal to the conditional probability of S given not-S or P, that is:

$$R(S) = \epsilon/Pr(\sim S) + \epsilon$$

This quantity may be thought of as the cost, in terms of *relative* degradation of probability, of asserting a more specific statement. (Note that for an atomic sentence or a conjunction of atomic sentences, $S = P$ and $R(S) = Pr(S) = \epsilon$.)

This talk of *cost* in terms of *degradation of probability* may seem foreign to the foregoing informal discussion, but this is only because informal discussions conveniently neglect small probabilities. We talk as if I can assert that M. is in London with *exactly* as much confidence as I can assert that M. is in London or Singapore. But surely this is an idealization. There is some tiny probability that M. is in Singapore. Moving to a more specific assertion always incurs some cost in terms of degradation of probability. But if the costs are so tiny as to be negligible in the context at hand, the guiding principles of conversation tell us to go ahead and neglect them, and assert the more specific statement. But is the cost that is relevant here to conversational implicature absolute cost or relative cost?

We might plausibly be loath to forego asserting a statement S in favor of a more specific statement S' if that move would increase our chances of being wrong by a factor of 99 ($Res(S) = .99$), even if that chance of being wrong were still quite small. So suppose that I were almost certain that M. was in London, but also had excellent reasons to believe that, were he not, he would be in Singapore (pr(Singapore given not-London) $= .99$). Then would I be violating an implicature by asserting that he is in London or Singapore?

This is a delicate point, and in the fine tuning of the implicature may have to float with the context. Nevertheless, I am afraid that conversational implicature alone will not bridge the gap between the material conditional and the indicative conditional of ordinary language.

not. I have two main reasons. The first is that the cancelability test fails. The second is that conversational implicature cannot account for the asymmetry of roles of the consequent and the denial of the antecedent of a conditional.

As we have seen, cancellation of a conversational implicature is possible by giving fair warning that the rule in question is not to be followed. But anyone who has taught a class in elementary logic can testify that it is no simple matter to legitimate the material conditional as an account of the meaning of the English "if-then." Suppose I say, "I know where Moriarty is, but I'll only give you a clue. If he is in China, he is in Fukien Province," when my sole evidence for this assertion is my belief that he is in London. The cancellation does not perform the office of legitimization at all in the way it did in the original disjunctive example. And it scarcely helps if I blurt out, " . . . and my only evidence for this assertion is that I believe Moriarty to be in London." If anything should cancel the implicature, that should. But instead our feeling is that I asserted a conditional for which I had no evidence at all! Take a different sort of example. If I am ignorant with respect to the subsentences of a tautology, I can at least assert it (perhaps with an apologetic preamble). "Well, at least we know that there will be a sea battle tomorrow or there won't." But try the following on for size: "Well, at least we know that either if there is a sea battle the emperor of Persia will catch cold, or if the emperor of Persia catches cold there will be a sea battle." We do? But interpreting "if-then" in the foregoing as the material conditional makes it a tautology as well. I will not multiply examples here.[3] The point has, I think, been fairly made. There is something more basic than conversational implicature behind the divergence in the use of "if-then" and the material conditional.

I can highlight the point by saying where I think conversational implicature *does* operate with respect to in-

3. See E. Adams, *The Logic of Conditionals* (Dordrecht: Reidel, 1975) and W. Cooper, *Foundations of Logico-Linguistics* (Dordrecht: Reidel, 1978), ch. 8.

dicative conditionals. Consider the case where I assert a conditional solely on the basis of its consequent. I tell Holmes: "If Moriarty is in the Western Hemisphere, then he is in London." A bit misleading, if my sole evidence is evidence that he is in London, but I would hesitate to say false. Let us try the cancellation test: "I know where Moriarty is, but I will only give you a clue. If he is in the Western Hemisphere, then he is in London." Certainly that is a quite acceptable conversation. Here we have the asymmetry to which I alluded. The injunction that a conditional should not be asserted solely on the basis of evidence for the truth of its consequent is a *cancelable implicature*. The injunction that a conditional should not be asserted solely on the basis of evidence for the falsity of its antecedent is resistant to cancellation,[4] and thus cannot plausibly be simply the result of a general conversational implicature. Yet if the indicative conditional of conversation were the material conditional plus conversational implicature, the two would have to be on a par.

The idea of conversational implicature is very valuable. But though it illuminates some aspects of the indicative conditional, it leaves deeper-rooted problems unsolved. The indicative conditional is *not* the material conditional plus conversational implicature. It is *something else* plus conversational implicature. I shall call this unknown quantity the *basic assertibility value* of the conditional.[5]

IIA2. ASSERTIBILITY OF THE INDICATIVE CONDITIONAL GOES BY EPISTEMIC CONDITIONAL PROBABILITY PLUS CONVERSATIONAL IMPLICATURE.

The idea that the assertibility of the indicative conditional of natural language goes by the corresponding conditional

---

4. Of course, cancellability is a matter of degree. If we go to great enough lengths we can cancel almost any rule. See the discussions of cancellability in the references of note 1.

5. Grice also discusses *conventional* implicatures. I wish to assimilate any operative conventional implicatures into the basic assertibility value.

probability is so attractive that it has been advanced again
and again; we find it in Ramsey, Jeffrey, Ellis, Adams, and
Stalnaker. It explains neatly the asymmetry of consequent
and denial of antecedent that we noticed in the last section. The oddness of asserting a conditional simply on the
basis of evidence for its consequent, which we found to be
cancelable, can be given a Griceian explanation. It is misleading to assert "If p then q" when, despite the fact that
the conditional probability of q given p is high, p is statistically independent of, or even negatively relevant to, q:
for example, "If the Pirates try harder, they will not win
the pennant." But the implicature can be canceled, and
our language contains a variety of special devices for can-
celing by explicitly indicating the lack of positive statistical relevance of p to q:

> Although the Pirates try harder, they will not win
> the pennant.
> Even if the Pirates try harder, they will not win
> the pennant.
> If the Pirates try harder, they will nevertheless not
> win the pennant.

The *conditional probability hypothesis*, then, should
really read: *The assertibility of the indicative conditional
goes by epistemic conditional probability plus conversational implicature.* To remind ourselves of the quite different role of the denial of the antecedent, consider: "If I
win the lottery, I will be sad," asserted by someone *solely*
because he thinks that the chances of his winning are
miniscule. He has asserted something that he is not entitled to assert, and attempting to repair the damage by saying "Even if I win the lottery, I will be sad" doesn't help at
all. We must look at the conditional probability; the ratio
of the tiny probability of his winning and being sad to the
tiny probability of his winning. If this conditional probability is small, then even though the probability of the material conditional "I won't win, or I will be sad" is enormous, no amount of cancellation will allow us to assert
the indicative conditional. In short, in a contest between
conditional probability and probability of the material
conditional to fill the blank in the statement: "Assertibility of the indicative conditional goes by ———— plus con-

versational implicature," the probability conditional wins hands down.[6]

But there is another contender. In 1968 Stalnaker proposed a conditional whose truth conditions in a world were the truth conditions of the material condition in a selected possible world. The novel aspect of Stalnaker's modal approach is that the world selected is a function of the *antecedent* of the conditional in question (together with the world in which the truth of the conditional is being assessed). Intuitively, the selected world is that most similar to the actual world in which the antecedent is true. Thus the Stalnaker conditional also has that asymmetry between consequent and denial of antecedent

---

6. It would be nice if we could have a uniform way of treating basic assertibility—a uniform way of filling in the blank in the statement "assertibility goes by _____ plus conversational implicature." This is possible if we are willing to countenance truth value gaps. Following B. De Finetti (also N. Belnap), let us consider a conditional which has the same truth value as the consequent when the antecedent is true, but which lacks a truth value when the antecedent is false. (The disposition of the cases where the antecedent itself lacks a truth value can be handled in various ways, the simplest of which is to make the conditional lack a truth value in all such cases, and the most elegant of which is to use supervaluations.) And let us say that the basic assertibility value—what goes in the blank—is the *probability of truth, conditional on having a truth value.* (In Griceian terms, this can be thought of as a uniform way of building *conventional* implicatures into the basic assertibility value. On van Fraassen's account of presupposition, this amounts to taking the basic assertibility value as probability of truth conditional on fulfillment of presupposition.)

For ordinary two-valued sentences, the basic assertibility value is, as it should be, probability of truth. For the De Finetti–Belnap conditional $p \to q$, if p and q are themselves without truth value gaps, it is the conditional probability of q on p. The basic assertibility value (call it A) does not behave as a probability on sentences of the language that admit truth value gaps. For instance, we do *not* in general have $A(p \to q) = A(q)A(p \to q) + A(\sim q)A(p \to q)$, thus avoiding Lewis's triviality proof (see appendix 3). We do, however, have the following interesting consequences. If p, q, r do not themselves admit truth value gaps, then:

(Ramsey): $A(p \to q) = 1 - A(p \to \sim q)$

(Ellis): $A[p \to (q \to r)] = A[(p \& q) \to r]$

On the other hand, iteration in the antecedent brings trouble:

$A[(p \to q) \to p] = 1$

For a suggestion about how to handle interations in the antecedent, see appendix 3.

which we find in natural language but which the material
conditional lacks. The Stalnaker conditional shares with
the probability conditional the feature than an improbable
antecedent need not make it probable. Furthermore, the
Stalnaker conditional has the advantage of closure. The
truth value of a Stalnaker conditional in a world is defined
via the truth value of its components in selected worlds.
So, starting with a language whose sentences have well-
defined truth values, and given the appropriate selection
function, we can close the language under the formation
of new sentences by the Stalnaker conditional and truth
functions. But truth has not been defined for the probability conditional. We only have a basic assertibility value
for $p \to q$ of $Pr(q$ given $p)$. No sense has been given to
truth-functional compounds or iterations of conditionals.
We will discuss some attempts to extend the probability
conditional in appendix 3. But for the moment let us try to
compare the Stalnaker and probability conditionals in the
cases where they are both defined: single conditionals
whose antecedent and consequent are conditional-free.

How are we to make the comparison? Well, that depends on whether we take Stalnaker's theory strictly, as
consisting of the semantics with only the formal constraints on the selection function; or loosely, as incorporating the informal suggestions about the selection
function being based on resemblance and picking out a
minimally different world in which the antecedent is true.
Taken strictly, the Stalnaker theory *is* compatible with the
theory here proposed. What, then, is the heuristic value of
the idea that the selection function is based on comparative similarity? Let's test our intuitions on a familiar
example. I test my unknown simply by putting it in the
flame and see quite clearly and undeniably that it does not
burn yellow. I am reasonably sure that all sodium salts
burn yellow, so I am reasonably sure that in the most similar possible world to this in which it *is* a sodium salt, it
will burn yellow. (We can even have the sample spewed
out of a randomized sample selector just prior to the test,
to avoid quibbles about similarity in respect of how the
sample got there.) Nevertheless, I will affirm the indicative: "If this *is* a sodium salt, it did *not* burn yellow."

Examples of this kind can be multiplied: I see a man standing before me; I say, "If he *was* on Mars a second ago, he exceeded the speed of light." Here the conditional probability account is more illuminating than the idea of a selection function based on comparative similarity.

Examples are one thing, general principles another. Is there any reason to believe that the indicative conditional *always* coincides with the probability conditional (in the cases under consideration, where both are defined)? There is this. The competing theories agree that $Pr(p \& \text{If } P \text{ then } q) = Pr(p \& q)$. If we accept this as a governing principle for the English indicative conditional, then we can say:

> If the English indicative conditional is statistically independent of its antecedent, then the probability of the English conditional is equal to the conditional probability of its consequent on its antecedent.

Proof:

$$\text{Assume } Pr(\text{If } p \text{ then } q) = Pr\,[(\text{If } p \text{ then } q) \text{ given } p]$$
$$= Pr(p \& \text{If } p \text{ then } q)/Pr(p)$$
$$= Pr(p \& q)/Pr(p)$$
$$= Pr(q \text{ given } p)$$

I think it is a plausible hypothesis that the English indicative always *is* independent of its antecedent. What convinces me is that whatever lengths I go to to try to find a counterexample, the attempt always fails. Let's try for an example where the conditional is *dependent* on its antecedent, and a really powerful case where the existence of a very strong connection between antecedent and consequent depends on whether the antecedent is true or not: Suppose that there is a lump of sugar, and I do not know whether it has been put in water or not (say $Pr(W) = 1/2$). I am interested in the proposition "If it has been put in water, it has dissolved." In a desperate attempt to introduce a probabilistic dependence of the conditional on its antecedent, I introduce a belief in "Peirce's demon," who, when and only when the sugar is immersed in water, supplies just enough extra binding energy to render it insoluble. The "connection" between the antecedent and the consequent has most certainly been made dependent on whether the antecedent is true in the most dramatic possible way. But is the *English indicative* statistically dependent on its antecedent? The conditional probability, Pr(if it has been put in water, it has dissolved, *given* it has been put in water), is zero or close to it, owing to my belief in the mischievous demon. But the unconditional probability, Pr(if it has been put in water, it has dissolved), is equally low for the same reason. *The effects of the antecedent being true have already been discounted in evaluating the probability of the indicative conditional.* Evaluating the probability of the indicative conditional *given that* the antecedent is true, then, makes no change. But when this is true, the conditional is statistically independent of its antecedent, and the probability of the conditional is the corresponding conditional probability.

IIA3. HOW LAWS SUPPORT INDICATIVE CONDITIONALS

If uniterated indicative conditionals are thought of in the way I suggested in the last section, we can give a nice account of how and when they are supported by well-confirmed laws. Universal laws are, by the analysis in section IB9, confirmed according to the epistemic expectation of *objective* resiliency.[7] A well-confirmed law will usually have high *epistemic* resiliency as well, but we can contrive cases where epistemic resiliency is low while a law is well confirmed: the unknown sample which burned green is such a case. Our theory predicts that here is a well-confirmed law, "All sodium salts burn yellow," which does not support the indicative conditional that instantiates it, "If this is a sodium salt, then it burns yellow." The law is well confirmed because there is a high expectation of objective resiliency; the conditional fails because it corresponds to a low epistemic conditional probability. The prediction that we should find such cases is satisfied and, using the theory as a guide, we can generate such cases at will.

In the more typical case where the material conditional which instantiates the law has high *epistemic* resil-

7. See section IB9.

iency, it follows immediately that the corresponding indicative conditional has a high basic assertibility value. In this case, however, we can tease a little more out of the account.

Let us say that a belief state (probability distribution) is, with respect to a conditional, If p then q:

> *factual* iff $Pr(p \& q) > .5$
> *semifactual* iff $Pr(\sim p \& q) > .5$
> *counterfactual* iff $Pr(\sim p_n \& \sim q) > .5$

Let us suppose that $Fa \supset Ga$ is resilient *simpliciter* (i.e., resilient over Boolean combinations of Fa and Ga) in the epistemic distribution. This not only guarantees that the conditional probability $Pr(Ga$ given $Fa)$ is high, but also gives us some information as to the statistical *relevance* of the antecedent Fa to the consequent Ga in these special cases:

> A. If $Fa \supset Ga$ is resilient *simpliciter* in a belief state, and the belief state is *counterfactual* with respect to If Fa then Ga, then Fa is *positively relevant* to Ga, i.e., $Pr(Ga$ given $Fa) > Pr(Ga$ given $\sim Fa)$.

Proof:

> If R $(Fa \supset Ga) > .5$
> Then $Pr(Ga$ given $Fa) > .5$
> But $Pr(Ga$ given $Fa) < .5$
> Since $Pr(\sim Ga \& \sim Fa) > .5$
> So $Pr(Ga$ given $Fa) > Pr(Ga$ given $\sim Fa)$.
> Note that in this case the full power of resiliency is not required to guarantee positive statistical relevance. All that is required in the counterfactual case is that the conditional probability $Pr(Ga$ given $Fa)$ be high.

Resiliency plays a fuller role in the following case:

> B. If $Fa \supset Ga$ is resilient *simpliciter* in a belief state and the belief state is *factual* with respect to the conditional, then Fa is *positively relevant* to Ga.

Proof:

> If positive relevance did not hold then
> $Pr(Ga$ given $\sim Fa) \geq Pr(Ga$ given $Fa)$
> $Pr(Ga \& \sim Fa)/Pr(\sim Fa) \geq Pr(Ga \& Fa)/Pr(Fa)$
> But by factuality $Pr(Fa \& Ga) > .5$

So $Pr(\sim Fa \ \& \ \sim Ga) < Pr(Fa \ \& \ \sim Ga)$
which contradicts
$R(Fa \supset Ga) > .5$

      C. In the *semifactual* case, unlike the two
           previous ones, $R(Fa \supset Ga) > .5$ does *not*
           guarantee positive statistical relevance of
           Fa to Ga.
           Example: $Pr(p \ \& \ q) = .2$
                          $Pr(p \ \& \sim q) = .1$
                          $Pr(\sim p \ \& \ q) = .5$

Note that if the law is *very* resilient we must go to
some lengths in minimizing $Pr(p)$ and $Pr(\sim q)$ to
get such an example. If $Pr(p)$ and $Pr(\sim q)$ are
bounded away from zero, then there is some point
as $R(p \supset q)$ approaches 1 where p must be positively relevant to q.

Even if a conditional is not a direct instantiation of a
law, the law together with suitable auxiliary information
can support the conditional. Suppose the law "Everything
that is both an F and a G is an H" is well confirmed and
that $Fa \ \& \ Ga \supset Ha$ is resilient in the epistemic distribution.

What is required of the auxiliary condition, Fa, so that
the conditional "If Ga then Ha is well confirmed? Some
light is thrown on the question by the following identity
of elementary probability theory:

        $Pr(Ha$ given $Ga) = Pr(Ha$ given $Fa \ \& \ Ga)Pr(Fa$
        given $Ga)$
        $+ Pr(Ha$ given $\sim Fa \ \& \ Ga)Pr(\sim Fa$ given $Ga)$

The sum can be viewed as a weighted average:

        $\alpha \, Pr(Ha$ given $Fa \ \& \ Ga) + (1 - \alpha) \, Pr(Ha$ given $\sim Fa$
        $\& \ Ga)$

The first term, $Pr(Ha$ given $Fa \ \& \ Ga)$ is vouchsafed by the
law in question. Now, of course, the second term, $Pr(Ha$
given $\sim Fa \ \& \ Ga)$, might also be high, in which case $Pr(Ha$
given $Ga)$ would be high no matter what the weighting.

But if this is not the case, $Pr(Ha$ given $Ga)$ can still be
high, provided that the first weighting factor, $\alpha = Pr(Fa$
given $Ga)$, is high enough. I will call this quantity the *contenability* of the Fa with Ga. Then high *cotenability of
the auxiliary condition* Fa *with the antecedent* Ga *of*

the conditional "If Ga then Ha" is a sufficient condition
for the law "Everything that is both an F and a G is an H"
to support the conditional.

In this more complex situation, positive statistical relevance again is guaranteed in a counterfactual situation,
but now it is no longer automatic in a factual situation
(unless the cotenability of Fa with Ga = 1).

A striking aspect of this probabilistic analysis of how
laws support conditionals is that in the counterfactual and
semifactual cases the auxiliary condition Fa need not itself be probable but only cotenable with the antecedent of
the conditional in question.

Suppose we are speculating on the fate of a match, a,
in our test chamber. The probability of the match being
dry is low, since it was selected at random from a batch
containing 90 percent wet matches. Nevertheless, the
cotenability of its being dry with its being scratched is
high, since a reliable assistant has been instructed to
scratch only dry matches. I assert with fair confidence: "If
match a has been struck, it has lit."

IIA4. THE PRIOR PROPENSITY ACCOUNT OF SUBJUNCTIVE
CONDITIONALS

It might be thought that subjunctives are mere stylistic
variants of indicatives, the counterfactual being used only
to convey the extra information that we are in a counterfactual belief state. There are striking examples which
suggest that this is not always the case.

The sodium salt example of the last section suggests
that basic assertibility of the subjunctive does not always
go by epistemic conditional probability, although basic
assertibility of the indicative does. We will maintain "If it
is a sodium salt, it didn't burn yellow," since it didn't, but
we will be quite confident in asserting "If it had been a
sodium salt, it would have burned yellow." Or consider
Adams's example: we will follow epistemic conditional
probability in asserting: "If Oswald didn't kill Kennedy,
then someone else did," but we will not follow it far
enough to assert: "If Oswald hadn't killed Kennedy, then
someone else would have." What has happened in these

examples is that the influence of any stable connection between the antecedent and consequent of the conditional
on the probability distribution has been swamped by our
quite certain knowledge about the truth value of the consequent in the absence of equally definitive knowledge of
the antecedent.

A natural suggestion, then, is that in evaluating the
subjunctive we should not look at the conditional probability in our *present* probability distribution, but rather
look at the conditional probability in a prior distribution
in which the perturbing knowledge of the truth value of
the consequent is suppressed. In our belief state prior to
putting the sample in the flame—that is, prior to conditionalizing on our observation that the sample didn't
burn yellow—the probability of its burning yellow conditional on its being sodium is indeed high. If we imagine a
belief state that includes our best knowledge of the events
leading up to the assassination but suppressing our
knowledge that it did in fact take place, we will find that
in that distribution our conditional probabilities coincide
with our degree of confidence in asserting the corresponding counterfactual.

Adams makes just this suggestion in "Prior Probabilities and Counterfactual Conditionals." He there points
out that in simple urn examples, where it is quite clear
what the appropriate prior is, the account gives just the
right results:

> Two urns, A and B, are filled with black and white
> balls, urn A containing .1% white and 99.9% black,
> urn B containing 50% of each color. One urn is
> selected at random and placed before an "observer"
> who draws one ball at random from it. This ball proves
> to be white.[8]

The probability that a black ball *would have been* drawn if
urn A *had* been selected is .999, while the probability that
a black ball *was* drawn if urn A *was* selected is zero.

8. E. Adams, "Prior Probabilities and Counterfactual Conditionals,"
in C. Hooker and W. Harper, eds., *Proceedings of International Congress
on the Foundations of Statistics* (Dordrecht: Reidel, 1975).

Exactly what the correct prior is in more complicated cases, as in the preceding examples, is not so precisely specified. This is, in fact, the locus of the ambiguity of the counterfactual on the prior probability account.

But although the epistemic prior probability theory of counterfactuals gives a credible account on these examples, it cannot be quite right. Consider Adams's counterexample to his own theory:

Imagine the following situation. We have just entered a room and are standing in front of a metal box with two buttons marked 'A' and 'B' and a light, which is off at the moment, on its front panel. Concerning the light we know the following. It may go on in one minute, and whether it does or not depends on what combinations of buttons A and B, if either, have been pushed a short while before, prior to our entering the room. If exactly one of the two buttons has been pushed then the light will go on, but if either both buttons or neither button has been pushed then it will stay off. We think it highly unlikely that either button has been pushed, but if either or both were pushed then they were pushed independently, the chances of A's having been pushed being 1 in a thousand, while the chances of B's having been pushed is a very remote 1 in a million. In the circumstances we think there is only a very small chance of 1,000,999 in one billion (about 1 in a thousand) that the light will go on, but a high probability of 999 in a thousand that *if B was pushed, the light will go on.*

Now suppose that to our surprise the light does go on, and consider what we would infer in consequence. Leaving out numerical probabilities for the moment, we would no doubt conclude that the light probably lit because A was pushed and B wasn't, and not because B was pushed and A wasn't. Therefore, since A was probably the button pushed, *if B had been pushed the light wouldn't have gone on,* for then both buttons would have been pushed. *The point here is that the counterfactual would be affirmed a posteriori in spite of the fact that the corresponding indicative was very improbable a priori*, because its contrary "if B was pushed then the light will go on" had a probability of .999 *a priori*.[9]

My suggestion is that the prior probability account can be saved by one small change—the probabilities involved are the prior *propensities* rather than the prior epistemic probabilities—with the relation between the two being taken as in part 1 of this book. If we do not know for certain the values of the prior propensities, we may have to do with a weighted average—the expected prior propensities. The weights in this average will be epistemic probabilities, and we should use the best ones available—for this job—the *posterior* epistemic probabilities. I will use PR for epistemic probabilities, pr for propensities, and BAV for basic assertibility value. I will use the superscripts i and f for prior (initial) and posterior (final) respectively. Let the double arrow, $\Rightarrow$, symbolize the subjunctive conditional. Then the theory that I am suggesting can be succinctly expressed thus:

$$***BAV(p \Rightarrow q) = \sum_j PR^f[pr_j^i] \cdot pr_j^i(q \text{ given } p)$$

where the pr_j^is are the appropriate prior propensity distributions.

Let us analyze Adams's example according to this theory. Letting $A = A$ was pushed, $B = B$ was pushed, and $L =$ the light goes on, the counterfactual to be analyzed is $B \Rightarrow L$. The relevant prior propensities depend on whether A was pushed or not and are gotten by conditionalizing out on these two alternatives: $pr_A^i(p) = PR^i(p \text{ given } A)$; $pr_{\sim A}^i(p) = PR^i(p \text{ given } \sim A)$. The values of $PR^f[pr_A^i] = PR^f(A)$ and $PR_A^f[pr_{\sim A}^i] = PR^f(\sim A)$ are gotten by Bayes's theorem. The happy result is that $BAV(B \Rightarrow L)$ as defined by $***$ is appropriately small as desired, as a consequence of the high *posterior* epistemic probability of the prior propensities associated with A being pushed. Adams, in fact, gives an "ad hoc two-factor model" for his example which is equivalent to the analysis forthcoming from the prior propensity approach. But from this point of view, Adams's model is not ad hoc but entirely natural. Suppose

9. E. Adams, *The Logic of Conditionals* (Dordrecht: Reidel, 1975).

that each of the prior propensity distributions can be identified with a physical foundation K_j (in the preceding example, the foundations for the two propensity distributions are A and $\sim A$). Then *** could be rewritten as:

$$BAV(p \Rightarrow q) = \sum_j PR^f(K_j) PR^i(q \text{ given } p \& K_j)$$

a form that we shall meet again in the discussion of rational decision. Where p and q lie in the future, we can usually take $PR^i = PR^f$. In other cases, such as the ones just cited, there is a natural choice for the appropriate prior. But it should come as no surprise that choice of the appropriate prior may be less than routine. All the vaguenesses and ambiguities of the subjunctive still exist.[10]

The prior probability account of the subjunctive no longer shares with the Stalnaker conditional the principle that $Pr(\text{If } p \text{ then } q) > Pr(p \& q)$. We have to stretch a little to put this difference to the test, but we do find some examples when we consider what Adams calls the *explanatory use* of the counterfactual.

> Mr. Snerd: Why is the floor dirty?
>
> Mrs. Snerd: If someone had just walked all over it with muddy boots, it would be dirty, wouldn't it?
>
> etc.

If Mrs. Snerd were using a Stalnaker conditional, she might, with at least as great justification, have said "If God made little green apples, the floor would be dirty" or "If $2 + 2 = 4$, the floor would be dirty."

One might take the position that the explanatory use is a pathological use of the counterfactual, but I prefer a treatment which can assimilate it, in a nontrivial way.

There is another way in which this account differs from the classical Stalnaker account with respect to chance processes. Suppose I flip a coin and it comes up heads (or a particle decays in one of several possible

---

10. Choice of the appropriate prior may depend on the individuation of the relevant chance process. A slot machine comes up three pears. Would we say: "If the left wheel had come up apple, the other two would (still) have come up pears"? It depends on whether we think of the play of the slot machine as a single chance process, or as consisting of three separate chance processes. (This explains the "spinner" example in Adams, *Logic of Conditionals*, pp. 132–33.)

ways). Consider the conditional: "If I had flipped the coin a millisecond earlier, it would have come up heads" ("If the particle had decayed a millisecond earlier, it would have decayed in the same way"). On the idea of similarity of possible worlds in which the antecedent is true, these conditionals should be *as strongly assertible as any*: making the consequent true picks up similarity at no cost. But intuitively this counterfactual is not so unproblematic. (The example can be made more extreme, if need be, by considering the case in which an extremely improbable outcome of the chance process has taken place.) The prior propensity account which gives this counterfactual a basic assertibility value of one-half is more in line with ordinary usage than the Stalnaker account which would presumably give it a probability near 1.[11]

11. The two preceding sorts of examples might be accommodated within the general Stalnaker approach by considering Stalnaker conditionals with propensity-attributing consequents:

   If p then $pr(q) = a$

Then I could fairly say of the coin that if it had been flipped a millisecond ago, the probability of its coming up heads would have been one-half, and it need not be the case that for any true statements, p, q, if p then $pr(q) = 1$; hence the explanatory use of counterfactuals need not be trivialized. That approach is consistent with the approach I have suggested. If K_js form a partition for physical bases for propensities, then if K_i is the true member of the partition, we could take as the correct value for a in the foregoing conditional:

   $PR(q$ given p & $K_i)$

This, however, would still leave the conditional with unqualified consequent—"If this coin had been flipped a millisecond ago, it would have come up heads"—assertible alongside the conditional with probabilistic consequent—". . . would have had a fifty-fifty chance of coming up heads." The proponent of the Stalnaker approach might deal with this remaining deviation from usage by maintaining that we blur the distinctions between probabilistic consequents and take as the assertibility value of a subjunctive with an unqualified consequent, the expected value of the probability of the consequent of the true conditional with probabilistic consequent. The story would then be that the conditional with unqualified consequent is not being used literally, but rather doing useful duty as a carrier for an expectation. Under these gratuitous proposals, the Stalnaker approach can be made to agree with the prior propensity approach with regard to assertibility values of subjunctive conditionals with either unqualified or probabilistic consequents.

IIA5. How Laws Support Subjunctive Conditionals

It follows from the treatment of confirmation of laws and basic assertibility value of subjunctives I have advocated that well-confirmed laws always support their subjunctive instantiations, even in cases where the corresponding indicatives are not supported. Thus we affirm: "If this had been a sodium salt, it would have burned yellow"; "If you had been on Mars a second ago, you wouldn't be here now," and so forth.

The connections that held for indicatives between factuality, counterfactuality, and semi-factuality of belief state, on the one hand, and statistical relevance of the antecedent of the conditional to its consequent, on the other, do not hold, in general, for subjunctives. Factuality or counterfactuality of my current epistemic probabilities with respect to a conditional need not be reflected as factuality or counterfactuality in the relevant prior propensity distributions. Conversely, neither the resiliency of $Fa \supset Ga$, nor the probability of Ga conditional on Fa, need be high in the current epistemic distribution for the counterfactual "If Fa had been the case, then Ga would have been" to be assertible (as is shown by the example of the sodium salt). This might lead us to believe that for subjunctives (as distinguished from indicatives) we can find examples where the conditional is assertible, where the current epistemic distribution is counterfactual with respect to it, and where, in the current epistemic distribution, the antecedent of the conditional is not positively statistically relevant to its consequent. Adams's two button example, which was discussed in the last section, is just such a case. On the other hand, in those cases where the correct propensity distribution is known and where the antecedent and consequent of the conditional both lie in the future, it is usually plausible to take the current epistemic distribution as the operative prior propensity distribution, and in those cases the analysis of section IIA3 goes over from indicatives to subjunctives unchanged.

The question of cotenability is also more complicated in the case of subjunctives than in the case of indicatives.

Of course, in the special cases described above the analysis goes over unchanged. But in general what is crucial for contenability is the probability of the auxiliary condition *Fa*, conditional of the antecedent of the conditional *Ga*, in the relevant prior propensity distributions. Let us call the epistemic expectation of this conditional probability the *subjunctive cotenability* of *Fa* with *Ga*. Then the subjunctive cotenability of *Fa* with *Ga* is simply the basic assertibility value of the subjunctive conditional "If *Ga* were the case, then *Fa* would be the case," just as Goodman originally suggested.[12] And we can show that we can make the basic assertibility value of the subjunctive. "If *Ga* were the case, *Ha* would be the case" as high as we please by making the law "Everything that is both an *F* and a *G* is an *H*" well enough confirmed, and by choosing the subjunctive cotenability of *Fa* with *Ga* high enough. Laws support subjunctives, on our analysis, in just the way everyone thinks they ought to.[13]

To summarize the results of our discussion of conditionals: *The basic assertibility value of simple uniterated conditionals, both indicative and subjunctive, is tied to conditional probability.* In the case of *indicative conditionals, it is conditional epistemic probability.* In the case of *subjunctives, it is conditional prior propensity,* if known, and, if this value is uncertain, its epistemic expectation.

For a discussion of iterated conditionals, see appendix 3.

12. Goodman, *Fact, Fiction and Forecast* 2d ed. (Indianopolis: Bobbs-Merrill, 1965), ch. 1.

13. At least everyone who (a) believes that laws support subjunctives which are direct instantiations of the law, and (b) subscribes to the principle that the following argument form is valid for subjunctives: If *p* were, then *q* would be; If *p* and *q* were, then *r* would be; therefore, If *p* were, *r* would be.

IIB Cause and Effect

Belief in the causal nexus is superstition.

Ludwig Wittgenstein
Tractatus Logico-Philosophicus 5.1361

---

*And what stronger instance can be produced of the sur-
prising ignorance and weakness of our understanding
than the present? For surely, if there be any relation
among objects which it imports to us to know perfectly, it
is that of cause and effect. On this are founded all our rea-
sonings concerning matters of fact or existence. By means
of it alone we attain any assurance concerning objects
which are removed from the present testimony of the
memory and the senses. The only utility of all sciences is
to teach us how to control and regulate future events by
their causes. Our thoughts and enquiries are, therefore,
every moment employed about this relation. Yet so imper-
fect are the ideas we form concerning it, that it is impossible to give any just definition of cause, except what is
drawn from something extraneous and foreign to it.*

David Hume
An Enquiry Concerning Human Understanding

IIB1. CAUSAL RELATIONS BETWEEN PHYSICAL PROPERTIES

---

*We may say that if A occurs in a larger proportion of cases
where B is than of cases where B is not, then will B also
occur in a larger proportion of cases where A is than of
cases where A is not; and there is some connection
through causation, between A and B.*

J. S. Mill
A System of Logic, bk. 3, ch. 17

After these general remarks on the nature of chance, we are prepared to consider in what manner assurance may be obtained that a conjunction between two phenomena, which has been observed a certain number of times, is not casual, but a result of causation, and to be received, therefore, as one of the uniformities of nature, though (until accounted for a priori) only as an empirical law.

We will suppose the strongest case, namely, that the phenomenon B has never been observed except in conjunction with A. Even then, the probability that they are connected is not measured by the total number of instances in which they have been found together, but by the excess of that number above the number due to the absolute frequency of A. If, for example, A exists always, and therefore co-exists with every thing, no number of instances of its co-existence with B would prove a connection; as in our example of the fixed stars. If A be a fact of such common occurrence that it may be presumed to be present in half of all the cases that occur, and therefore in half the cases in which B occurs, it is only the proportional excess above half that is to be reckoned as evidence toward proving a connection between A and B.

J. S. Mill
A System of Logic, bk. 3, ch. 17

But in general the statistician must, if he wishes to discuss adequately any case of statistical causation, take more than two variables into account. If, in the present illustration, a marked correlation be found to exist between rainfall and crop, this may conceivably be due to a mere relation between rainfall and temperature: the real nature of the relation between crop, rainfall, and temperature can only be discovered by dealing with all three at once. . . . The coefficient b_{12} then shows how much crop is on the average affected by a unit deviation from the average in rainfall when the temperature is constant, and the relation is not, therefore, subject to the possible misin-

terpretation noticed above. . . . The method can evidently be extended to any number of variables.

G. Udny Yule
"The Applications of the Method of Correlation to Social and Economic Statistics,"
International Statistical Institute Bulletin 18 (1910)

Such a mental partition is an indispensable first step. The order of nature, as perceived at first glance, presents at every instance a chaos followed by another chaos. We must decompose each chaos into single facts. We must learn to see in the chaotic antecedent a multitude of distinct antecedents, in the chaotic consequent a multitude of distinct consequents. This, supposing it be done, will not of itself tell us on which antecedents each consequent is dependent. To determine that point, we must endeavor to effect a separation of the facts from one another not in our minds only, but in nature. The mental analysis, however, must take place first. . . . The extent and minuteness of observation which may be requisite, and the degree of decomposition to which it may be necessary to carry the mental analysis, depend on the particular purpose in view. . . . In making chemical experiments we do not think it necessary to note the position of the planets; because experience has shown . . . that in such cases that circumstance is not material to the result.

J. S. Mill
A System of Logic, bk. 3, ch. 7

What does it mean to say that smoking is a (probabilistic) cause of lung cancer?

Mill tells us to look at a wide variety of combinations of prima facie causally relevant factors for the effect, E, and if we find one, C, such that when C is present E is present, and when C is absent E is absent, then we have grounds for believing that C causes E.[1] What is the correct application of Mill's methods to the probabilistic case? In

1. This is the double method of agreement.

the probabilistic case, the difference is not simply two-valued but rather, as Mill quite clearly sees,[2] a difference in the probability of the effect conditional on the cause: $Pr(E$ given $C)$ should be greater than $Pr(E$ given $\sim C)$. In other words, the cause should have positive statistical relevance to the effect. But the difference according to Mill's excellent intuition, should arise relative to each constellation of causally relevant background factors. So letting B_i by a maximal conjunction of relevant background factors, we are led to the Suppes-Cartwright characterization of probabilistic causality:[3]

$\quad$ *Suppes-Cartwright Condition (S.C.):*

$\quad\quad$ $PR(E$ given $C \& B_i) > Pr(E$ given $\sim C \& B_i)$ for all i

The probabilistic setting now makes for a subtlety that has no analogue in the two-valued case. It is possible that condition S.C. is satisfied even though C is not positively relevant to E overall; that is, even though $Pr(E$ given $C)$ is equal to or even less than $Pr(E$ given $\sim C)$. Suppose that air pollution got so bad that most people in the cities refrained from smoking out of sheer terror of putting their lungs in double jeopardy, while many people in areas of the countryside with relatively little pollution felt that they could allow themselves the luxury of smoking. Then the situation might quite well be such that:

$\quad\quad$ Pr (Lung cancer given smoking) $< Pr$(Lung cancer given not smoking)

although:

$\quad\quad$ Pr(Lung cancer given smoking & pollution) $>$ Pr(Lung cancer given not smoking & pollution)

$\quad\quad$ Pr(Lung cancer given smoking and no pollution) $> Pr$(Lung cancer given not smoking & no pollution)

because the intake of pollution is not statistically independent of smoking. Causal relevance is reflected in

$\quad$ 2. *A System of Logic*, 8th ed. (New York: Harper, 1874), bk. 3, ch. 17, secs. 2–3.

$\quad$ 3. Compare N. Cartwright, "Causal Laws and Effective Strategies," mimeographed (Stanford, 1978); P. Suppes, *A Probabilistic Theory of Causality* (Amsterdam: North Holland, 1970); W. Salmon, in *Statistical Explanation and Statistical Relevance* (Pittsburgh: Pittsburgh University Press, 1971); H. Reichenbach, *The Direction of Time* (Berkeley and Los Angeles: University of California Press, 1971).

statistical relevance *within* the cells of the partition by causally relevant background factors (the B_is), but the averaging which gives us the overall probability of lung cancer given smoking loses this causal information and gives a distorted picture of the causal situation. If you looked only at Pr(Cancer given smoking) vs. Pr(Cancer given not smoking), you might even come to the mistaken conclusion that smoking was a prophylactic against lung cancer. The negative correlation between smoking and lung cancer is a *spurious* correlation. A spurious correlation is one which disappears relative to other relevant factors; that is, ultimately, which disappears within the cells corresponding to maximal conjunctions of relevant background factors.[4]

One special case in which a spurious correlation disappears relative to a constellation of background factors, B_i, is when the correlated properties become *independent* within B_i, that is:

Reichenbach's Case of Screening-Off.[5]

$$Pr(E \text{ given } C \& B_i) = Pr(E \text{ given} \sim C \& B_i)$$

B_i is said to *screen off* C from E. (It follows that B_i also screens off E from C since statistical independence is symmetrical.) Reichenbach has in mind cases like the barometer and the rain. Although the falling barometer is prior to and positively correlated with the rain, it is not a cause of the rain but rather the effect of a common cause, certain meteorological conditions, M. This shows up in the statistics in that M screens off the falling barometer from the rain. But, as our example shows, *being screened off is only one way in which a spurious correlation may fail in the*

4. This idea was already explicitly formulated by F. Y. Edgeworth in 1892 and made use of by the English statistical school of Edgeworth, Pearson, and Yule thereafter. Much of Edgeworth's work had been anticipated half a century earlier in France by Bravais, but Edgeworth's paper of 1892 was written in ignorance of his contributions. See Edgeworth, "Correlated Averages," *Philosophical Magazine* 34 (1892):191–204; Edgeworth, "On the Application of the Calculus of Probabilities to Statistics," *International Statistical Institute Bulletin* (1910):537–51; Pearson, "Mathematical Contributions to the Theory of Evolution," *Proceedings of the Royal Society of London* 60 (1897):489–503; and Yule, "The Applications of the Method of Correlation to Social and Economic Statistics," *International Statistical Institute Bulletin* (1910):537–51.

5. *The Direction of Time*, ch. 4.

light of other causally relevant factors. An overall positive
correlation (between not smoking and getting cancer) can
turn into a negative one within each cell of the partition
according to causally relevant background factors, or an
overall negative correlation (between smoking and getting
cancer) may turn out to be an overall positive one in each
cell.

With these facts in mind, we can compare the
Suppes-Cartwright characterization of probabilistic causality with an alternative characterization, in terms of
screening-off. For instance, consider:
No-Screen Condition (NS):

(1) $Pr(E \text{ given } C) > Pr(E \text{ given } \sim C)$

and

(2) There is no W such that W screens off E from C
The *No-Screen* condition is seen to be defective in
several ways. Clause (1) is too strong. Clause (1) fails in
our example even though smoking is a probabilistic cause
of lung cancer. Clause (2) is both too strong and too weak.
The existential clause is too strong because statistical relevance may be averaged out; there may be a property that
screened off E from C, even though C is positively relevant
to E within every cell of the partition. It is too weak because spurious correlations can show up in ways other
than by screening-off. Positive correlations can change
into negative correlations within the cells, rather than to
independence. There is no screening-off in our example.

A plausible interesting weakening of condition S.C. is
a sort of Pareto-dominance kind of condition:

Pareto-Dominance Condition:

(1) $Pr(E \text{ given } C \text{ \& } B_i) \geq Pr(E \text{ given } \sim C \text{ \& } B_i)$ for every
   B_i

and

(2) $Pr(E \text{ given } C \text{ \& } B_i) > Pr(E \text{ given } \sim C \text{ \& } B_i)$ for some
   B_i in the fundamental partition

We may also, of course, consider notions such as causal
relevance relative to a set of fixed factors (a *ceteris paribus*
causal relevance), where we consider only those cells in
the partition in which the factors in question are present.
For instance, there might be a wonderfully efficient ciga-

rette filter which broke the connection between smoking and cancer, but which no one used because it was too expensive to manufacture. We might plausibly be interested in the connection of smoking and lung cancer holding the unavailability of filters fixed (which under the S.C. analysis reduces neatly to the question of whether smoking-without-filters is a probabilistic cause of lung cancer).

How does this analysis apply to causal factors for events? Here we want to fix the relevant factors that are *in fact present*.[6] A heart attack did cause poor Cecil's death. It is true that being run over by a steamroller screens off a heart attack from death, but Cecil was not, in fact, run over by a steamroller. We can neglect those cells which include being run over by a steamroller, and indeed the coroner would like to zero in on that cell which includes the true constellation of background causal factors. How does this type of analysis treat the notorious cases of overdetermination? Moriarty is simultaneously shot in the head by Holmes and Watson. (Assume Pr(death given Holmes's shot) = Pr(death given Watson's shot) = Pr(death given Holmes's and Watson's shots) = 1, just to make things nasty.) A faint air of paradox is generated by the fact that we can't say that either shot caused Moriarty's death. But that air is dispelled by the fact that we can say that the conjunction of the two factors did.

IIB2. Causal Chains of Physical Events

A clear distinction between open and closed systems is essential if confusion is to be avoided in discussing the problem of causality in physics.

Peter Havas
"Causality and Relativistic Dynamics," in Causality and Physical Theories

6. This is statistical relevance "objectified" in R. Jeffrey's sense (*The Logic of Decision* [New York: Macmillan, 1965]).

*Why do we prefer fields to action at a distance? The
answer is simple. We need fields to uphold the law of conservation of energy and momentum.*

Hans C. Ohanian
Gravitation and Spacetime

---

*Bell's Theorem is the most profound discovery of sci-
ence. It shows that if the statistical predictions of quantum theory are approximately correct, then, in certain
cases, the principle of local causes must fail.*

H. P. Stapp
"Bell's Theorem and the World Process," in Il Nuovo
Cimento

The fundamental laws of physics are never of the
form "Smoking causes lung cancer," and one might be
tempted to agree with Russell that the notion of cause is
something to be outgrown in science.[7] But we do find a
conception of cause playing a fundamental role in one
area of physics: relativity theory.[8] Two events are causally
connectable if they can be connected by a *causal chain* or
signal. What is the fundamental notion of causal chain
that is operative here? There are paradigms, but I have
been unable to find any explicit definition or analysis that

    7. "On the Notion of Cause," in *Mysticism and Logic and Other Es-
says* (London: George Allen and Unwin, 1950).
    8. See J. Ehlers, F. A. E. Pirani, and A. Schild, "The Geometry of
Free Fall and Light Propagation," in L. O'Raifeartaigh, ed., *General Rel-
ativity: Essays in Honor of J. L. Synge* (London: Oxford University Press,
1972); A. Grünbaum, *Philosophical Problems of Space and Time*, 2d ed.
(Boston: Reidel, 1974); S. Hawking and G. Ellis, *The Large Scale Struc-
ture of Space-Time* (Cambridge: Cambridge University Press, 1973), ch. 6;
R. W. Latzer, "Non-Directed Light Signals and the Structure of Time,"
Synthese 24:236–80; D. Malament, "Causal Theories of Time and the
Conventionality of Simultaneity," *Nous*, vol. 11, no. 3 (1977):293–99;
C. Misner, K. Thorne, and J. A. Wheeler, *Gravitation* (San Francisco:
Freeman, 1973), 16.5; H. Ohanian, *Gravitation and Space-Time* (New
York: Norton, 1976), ch. 5; and Zeeman, "Causality Implies the Lorentz
Group," *Journal of Mathematical Physics* 5 (1964):490–93.

is very enlightening. The paradigms are: world line of a particle; path of a sharp fronted wave front; path of a light ray. These paradigms have some important features in common. They represent transfers of energy-momentum; they can be used to transfer information. But can we say anything deeper about the concept of a causal chain? I believe we can: the concept of a causal chain seems to be closely tied to our needs for symmetry and invariance in our scientific view of the world.

Conservation laws are fundamental to physics. They are the hallmarks of symmetries in the fundamental laws of nature. But there are lots of physical systems for which the requisite quantities are not conserved; these are not thought of as counterexamples to conservation laws, because they are considered *open* systems. The conservation laws hold strictly only for *closed* systems. Thus the distinction between open and closed systems is fundamental to our conception of the world as governed by laws having a high degree of symmetry. Open and closed to what? The most natural general answer is: *to cause and effect.* In particular cases, this "metaphysical" notion of cause is given a precise meaning by the physical theory involved. Any injection or withdrawal of a quantity which the theory says is conserved will count as opening the system. From this viewpoint, a causal influence can be thought of as consisting in the transmission of a normally conserved quantity. A causal chain through a system can be viewed as a chain of subsystems with broken conservation laws, such that conservation can be recaptured by considering a system broad enough to include the whole chain. This conception of cause is, then, integral to the enterprise of finding the maximum amount of order in the phenomena.

In a theory in which mass and energy are separate quantities, each of which is conserved, we have correlative notions of material and efficient causes.[9] The special theory of relativity has achieved a unification of the concepts of material cause and efficient cause via the concept of energy-momentum.

9. Belief in the conservation of entropy would yield a kind of *formal* cause as a correlative notion.

Locality

Let us concentrate our attention on the special case within special relativity where causal chains are thought of as transfers of energy-momentum. Then the special theory also throws a good deal of light on the physical status of an old physical-philosophical chestnut: action at a distance versus spatiotemporal continuity in the propagation of causal influence. Can energy-momentum be transferred from a body to a distant body without residing in any intermediated substance (action at a distance) or must it be transmitted via a continuous path between the two (local action)? The idea of action at a distance, though certainly logically consistent, has been repugnant to the physical intuitions of thinkers from Democritus to Einstein. The author of the most successful action-at-a-distance theory in the history of physics did not like it. In a famous passage from the third letter to Bentley, Newton writes:

> It is inconceivable that inanimate brute Matter should without the mediation of something else which is not material, operate upon, and effect other Matter without mutual Contact. . . . That gravity should be innate, inherent and essential to Matter so that one body may act upon another at a Distance thro' a Vacuum without the mediation of anything else, by and through which their Action and Force may be conveyed from one to the other, is to me so great an Absurdity that I believe that no Man who has in philosophical Matters a competent Faculty of thinking can ever fall into it.[10]

But although Newton's physical intuition balked at action at a distance, his dynamics permitted it. In particular, it did not conflict with the principle of conservation of energy. Let body A lose a certain amount of energy at a time t, and another distant body acquire it at t, and conservation of energy of the system is satisfied.

It is not so easy for action-at-a-distance theories to satisfy conservation of energy-momentum in special rela-

10. Quoted in H. Ohanian, *Gravitation and Space-Time*.

tivity, the fundamental reason being that there is no absolute simultaneity relation. Two particles have world lines
that do not intersect. One loses energy-momentum at
some point on its world line. When does the other get it?
These considerations lead to a remarkable "no-interaction
theorem" of van Dam and Wigner. Consider a system of
two particles whose world lines do not intersect (figures 2
and 3). Suppose that there is nothing *else* in the system
that is storing energy-momentum, that is to say, that the
energy-momentum of the system is the sum of the
energy-momenta of the particles. And suppose that the
energy-momentum of the system is Lorentz invariant.
Then if the energy-momentum of the system is constant,
the energy-momentum of *each particle* is constant. In
other words, there is *no causal interaction without contact*. Where there appears to be causal interaction between
particles without contact, we need *the field* to store
energy-momentum, so that what appeared to be a particle
system becomes a particle-plus-field system. Reapplying
the van Dam–Wigner argument *to the field itself,* we see
that the field must transmit energy-momentum *continuously* through the field. The principle of the spatiotemporal continuity of causal chains is thus seen to
be intimately linked with conservation of energy-
momentum and the Minkowskian structure of space-
time.[11]

It follows that relativistically invariant action-at-a-
distance theories are possible only at the cost of violation
of the principle of conservation of energy-momentum. If
we are willing to bear this cost, we can replace a relativistically invariant local field theory with a relativistically invariant action-at-a-distance particle theory.
One can, furthermore, get something that formally resem-
bles conservation of energy-momentum, by defining a
quantity for a system of particles that depends not only on
the energy-mementa of the particles but also on something called "interaction momentum" (an extra fudge

11. The same considerations apply in the general theory in that
space-time is locally Minkowskian and energy-momentum is locally
conserved.

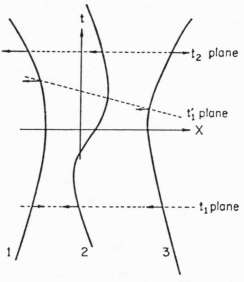

Figure 2. Interpretation of Eq. (11). The world lines of particles 1, 2, and 3 are assumed to be coplanar and to lie entirely in the x-t plane. The x components of the momenta of three particles are shown at times t_1 and t_2; their sum must be equal because of the conservation law for linear momentum. It follows, however, from (11) that the sum of these components is the same also if taken on the t_1' plane, which represents the points that are simultaneous from the point of view of any other coordinate system. (From H. van Dam and E. P. Wigner, "Instantaneous and Asymptotic Conservation Laws for Classical Relativistic Mechanics with Interacting Point Particles," *Physical Review* 142 (1966):840.)[*Author's Note:* Equation 11 says that the sum of the linear momenta of the particles is the same along each plane of simultaneity. It derives from the assumption that the components of the system momentum transform as a vector, together with the assumptions that in each Lorentz frame the components of the system momentum are gotten by summing the components of the particle momenta at simultaneous points, and that the components of the system momentum are conserved.]

term). We know from our local field theory that if we can arrange for the interaction momentum to equal the value of the field momentum in the field theory, the total quantity for the system of particles will be conserved. We know from our local field theory how to write the energy-momentum of the field in terms of the past history of the

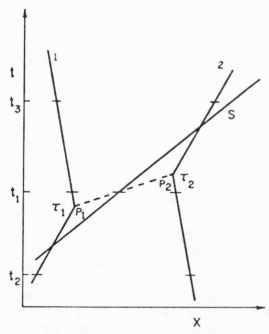

Figure 3. World lines of two interacting particles with equal masses. Linear momentum Δ leaves particle 1 at P_1 and arrives at particle 2 at P_2. The sum of the linear momenta must be the same at t_2, t_1, and t_3. Hence, an interaction momentum must be present at t_1; its x component is positive. Similarly, an interaction momentum must be present in the coordinate system in which the points of the line S are simultaneous; its x component is negative. (From van Dam and Wigner, "Instantaneous and Asymptotic Conservation Laws," p. 841.)

particles that contributed to the field. So we can write relativistically invariant action-at-a-distance theories that give the same predictions for particles as their local field-theory counterparts, and that contain a formal analogue of conservation of energy-momentum. Nevertheless, I do not think that such a picture takes the conservation law seriously as a physical principle. The interaction momentum is treated as a formal rather than a physical quantity. To see this clearly, consider the cases where a particle and an antiparticle annihilate. Energy-momentum is conserved as interaction momentum, but now there is nothing in the physical ontology of the theory with which

the interaction momentum can be associated.[12] We have
ample reason from the history of physics to argue that
conservation of energy-momentum should be taken seriously, as a physical principle, requiring physical bearers
for the quantities involved. I believe, then, that we have
strong evidence for the reality of the field and for the
locality of causal chains which represent the transfer of
energy-momentum.

Tachyons

What of the possibility that causal chains may exceed the
speed of light? There has been some discussion of the
theoretical possibility of *tachyons,* particles whose world
lines fall outside the null cone. Again, Lorentz invariance
by itself does not rule out the existence of tachyons, but it
does lead to rather awkward consequences for tachyons
that do not follow for slower particles. The basic problem
appears already in kinematic considerations. What is the
4-velocity of a tachyon? Whereas *tardyons* (slower than
light) and *luxons* (speed of light) inherit an unambiguous
orientation (a "future" direction) from the orientation of
the light cones, tachyons do not. Give a tachyon an orientation and it will be future-directed in one Lorentz frame
and past-directed in another. This leaves only two possibilities: (1) Tachyons come with an orientation that *is*
invariant. It is a consequence of this view that in some
Lorentz frames particles travel backward in time, and the
direction of causation is from future to past. It is also well
known that this opens the door to causal loops—closed
causal chains. (2) In order to avoid the aberrant causal behavior that results under (1), it has been suggested that
orientation for tachyons should be frame-dependent
rather than absolute, with the tachyon taking its
orientation-in-a-frame as the future direction in that
frame. Thus, what in one frame would look like *A* emitting a particle and *B* absorbing it would, in another, look
like *B* emitting and *A* absorbing. The closed causal chains
of possibility (figure 4, *above*) are avoided by reversing

12. See H. Ohanian, *Gravitation and Space-Time,* p. 40.

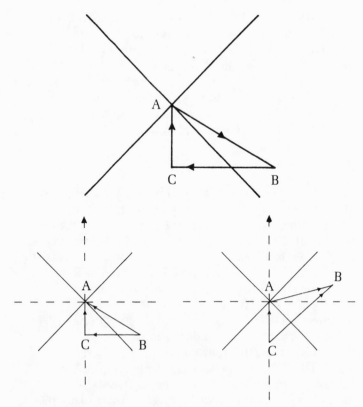

Figure 4. Tachyons forming a closed causal chain.

The situation of the above as it appears in two reference frames, with orientation being frame-dependent.

the direction of certain subchains, but of *different* sub-chains in *different* reference frames (figure 4, *below*). It would perhaps be too fine a point to ask here the logicians' question: "What orientation is given to a tachyon in a frame in which it lies along the plane of simultaneity?" But it is worth emphasizing that *this alternative deprives the direction of causation of its absolute character* and reduces it to a frame-dependent status.

If one holds as well-confirmed physical principles both that there are no closed causal chains and that orientation is frame-independent, then tachyons are already ruled out on kinematic grounds. If tachyons are ruled out, either for these reasons or for dynamical ones, and if the position I have suggested with regard to action-at-a-distance theories is correct, we then have as a well-confirmed *contingent physical principle* that causal chains (energy-momentum causal chains) are spatiotemporally continuous and only connect events with a timelike or lightlike separation.

Asymmetry

In relativity theory, each causal chain is assumed to be endowed with a *direction* (an orientation), so there *is* an asymmetric causal relation in the area. We may think of the direction as "pointing toward the future," where *future* is used in a local sense, or as "pointing from cause to effect." But if a space-time model is allowed by the theory, reversing all the arrows gives a space-time model which is equally allowed. *The theory does not distinguish between the direction of cause to effect and the direction of effect to cause.* What one cannot do is simply reverse *some* of the directions, so that they do not mesh properly. There is a world of difference between A and B in figure 5. One cannot regard the heavy line in the Minkowski space of figure 6 as one causal chain joining two spacelike separated events! (Causal connectability is not transitive.) Thus, we may say that relativity demands that there be an asymmetric causal relation—A is *forward*-causally-connectable to B, although it does not provide the means for distinguishing that relation from its inverse.

Relativistic dynamics, then, throws a good deal of light on causal connectability, but it fails to give a full explanation of the asymmetry of the causal relation. The theory requires that there be an asymmetric causal relation, but it underdetermines orientability even in the nicest case (Minkowski space-time), in such a way that it cannot tell us how to distinguish the relation of cause to effect from the inverse relation of effect to cause. On the other hand, it would be wrong to say that relativistic considerations provide no constraints on the asymmetry. In Minkowski space, to pick an orientation for one light cone

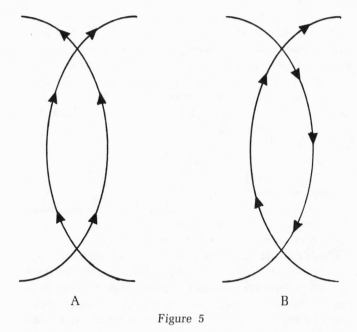

Figure 5

is to pick an orientation for them all, since the orientations must mesh together. This raises the possibility of a global, cosmological solution to the problem. One might find the arrow from cause to effect in some global asymmetry, rather than taking the more obvious path and looking for it locally. In the most pathological examples of general

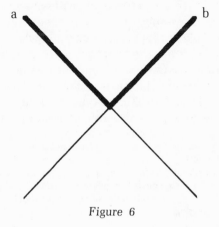

Figure 6

relativistic space-times, these advantages are all lost. In fact, there exist examples of "non—temporally orientable" space-times where things will not mesh at all (i.e., where it is impossible "to define *continuously* a division of non-spacelike vectors into two classes, which we arbitrarily label future and past directed."[13] But these are curiosa rather than live candidates for our universe. Of more real interest is the possibility of space-time singularities at black holes. Excepting such possible singularities, the requirement that orientations mesh continuously does promote the problem from a local to a global one for most physically plausible space-times.

Where, then, is the physical foundation for the asymmetry which is such a basic feature of our ordinary conception of cause and effect? With the exception of some elementary particle interactions (neutral K meson decay), none of our basic physical theories is time-asymmetric.[14] Moreover, whatever the time asymmetries of meson decay, they do not appear to be responsible for the asymmetries of everyday experience that shape our ordinary conception of cause and effect. The familiar time asymmetries of macrophenomena are due to asymmetries in the initial conditions in two basic kinds of physical theory: electrodynamics and statistical mechanics. Light a match, and a coherent spherical shell of radiation travels outward until it contacts other objects; throw a pebble into a still pond, and coherent water waves radiate out to the shore. The temporal inverses of these processes are permitted by theory, but are never observed. Such is the de facto time asymmetry of electrodynamics. Pour cold water into a cup of coffee and a little while later the contents of the cup will have come to a uniform temperature; shuffle a deck of cards initially arranged in suits and they will become mixed; give a speech in Times Square and the structure of your words will be quickly lost in interaction with the

13. See S. Hawking and G. Ellis, *The Large Scale Structure of Space-Time* (Cambridge: Cambridge University Press, 1973), ch. 6.
14. Here the time symmetry, T, is replaced by a weaker symmetry involving charge and parity, the PCT symmetry. See P. C. W. Davies, *The Physics of Time Asymmetry* (Berkeley and Los Angeles: University of California Press, 1977).

surrounding noise. The temporal inverses of these processes are never experiences, even though the underlying
theory is time-symmetric. Given a low-entropy, or-
ganized, information-laden state to start with, the theory
predicts that in all probability the system will evolve to a
higher-entropy, more disorganized, less informed, more
probable state. (Note that this is perfectly consistent with
the time symmetry of the theory. If it were given that the
system ends in a low entropy state, then the theory predicts with equal force that it came from a higher entropy
state.) Such are the de facto thermodynamic asymmetries.

There are two sorts of theoretical models of the universe which explain these asymmetries: the universe as a
closed box and the universe as an infinite sink. On the first
sort of model, there is even a way to reduce the elec-
trodynamic asymmetry to the thermodynamic one by in-
voking thermodynamic asymmetry for the walls of the
box.[15] On the second model, the two asymmetries arise in
similar ways: initial conditions give initial concentrations
of something which is then dissipated into an infinite
sink. (Some physicists hold that the temporal asymmetries of measurement in quantum mechanics are also thermodynamic in character.) It is only at this level that
physics finally allows us to complete the story of the
asymmetry of the causal relation. The direction from
cause to effect is the direction of increasing entropy and
decreasing order and information. The effect, if you
please, has less perfection than the cause. That this is so is
contingent, de facto, and statistical.

Statistical Indications of Locality

Let us now take another look at macroscopic causal chains
from a thermodynamic point of view. Our fundamental
partition is now limited to macroproperties, and let us
suppose that from the macroscopic point of view our
causal chain is like a current of information in a sea of

15. See J. A. Wheeler and R. Feynman, "Interaction with the Ab-
sorber as the Mechanism of Radiation," *Reviews of Modern Physics* 17
(1945):157–81.

noise. If we choose our viewpoint and our cases so that
causal chains look like messages traveling along noisy
channels, then the state-of-the-message event at one point
in the chain will be more closely correlated with near
state-of-the-message events than with far ones because of
the random nature of the noise which degrades the message. And if event C is between events A and B it will
screen off one from the other. This has nothing to do with
temporal order, but rather with betweenness in the chain.
It even works for branching chains. Suppose that the
channel branches. Then the message along both branches
will be degraded, but in all likelihood in different ways,
because of the random character of the noise. So the
state-of-the-message event at the node will screen off the
state-of-the-message events on one branch from those on
another. (Likewise for the temporal inverse of this process.) Thus, in cases where these assumptions apply, the
screening-off relation captures for us, in a crude, macroscopic, and statistical way, what we already have independently, in a more precise form, and with less assumptions from dynamics: the betweenness relations
among events on a causal chain.[16]

Locality Reconsidered: Quantum Mechanics

At the level of quantum theory, questions of locality are
conceptually delicate. The issues involved can be elucidated by examination of a version of the paradox of Einstein, Podolsky, and Rosen.

A spin-0 particle decays into two spin-1/2 particles.
After the particles are spatially separated (as far as you
please), they encounter measuring apparatus which determines spin in a selected direction.[17] We may imagine
the apparatus to be rotatable, so that the direction in
which spin is to be measured can be chosen just before
measurement, when the particles are already widely separated. A measurement for one particle will, according to

16. Compare Reichenbach's discussion in ch. 4 of The Direction of
Time.
17. The spin measurement can also localize the particle, so it is
legitimate to speak of spatial separation at the time of measurement.

quantum theory, instantaneously collapse the wave function for the two-particle system. By conservation of spin, determination of spin +1 in a specified direction for one particle is determination of spin −1 in the specified direction for the other.

Our measurement on the left particle has collapsed the wave function of the two-particle system. Certain aspects of the collapse are reassuring. Our measurement has not succeeded in transferring energy-momentum from one particle to another. Nor can I, stationed at the left-hand measuring apparatus, use my measurement to send a signal to my comrade, stationed at the right-hand measuring apparatus. For his probability of getting +1 in the measurement in the direction he chooses, given that I have performed a measurement in the direction I chose (but not given the results of that measurement), is still one-half!

On the other hand, if my friend and I choose the same direction, then if my measurement yields +1 his will yield −1. How are the probabilities at his end instantaneously affected by the outcome of a random experiment at my end? The collapse of the wave function is a physical process which is not relativistically invariant. That the collapse of the wave function is a *physical* process, and not merely an epistemological one, is a central principle of quantum mechanics. Collapse of the wave function wipes out cross terms and thus possible interference effects. Interference effects are physically observable.

If collapse of the wave function were merely epistemological, there would be no trouble. Suppose two pieces of paper, one marked "up" and one marked "down," are put into separate boxes; my friend and I choose boxes at random, carry them in opposite directions, and open them. Here we have a correlation of spacelike separated events which can be traced back to a *local* common cause. Partitioning according to the common cause screens off, à la Reichenbach, the probabilistic relevance of one event to the other.[18] The situation in quantum mechanics is *not* like this. The collapse of the wave function *is* a physical process. There *is* no common

18. See the previous subsection.

cause to explain the correlation between spacelike separated events.

Some thinkers have hoped that the cases treated by quantum mechanics might ultimately be treated by means of a hidden variables theory, wherein a hidden variable, λ, supplies the "common cause," and thus assimilates these cases to that of the two boxes. In an analysis of the Einstein-Podolsky-Rosen paradox in 1965, Bell proved a theorem showing that any deterministic, local, hidden variables theory must disagree in its *predictions* with quantum mechanics. Bell's theorem has been generalized to stochastic hidden variables theories by Bell himself and by Clauser and Horne.[19]

As we have seen, there is more than one sense of locality available, so it will be of interest to see what sense or senses are at issue in these proofs. One principle of locality can be stated in terms of functional independence.[20] Let the left-hand experimenter choose the orientation of his apparatus so as to perform experiment E_{11} or E_{12} and the right-hand experimenter choose the orientation of his apparatus so as to perform experiment E_{21} or E_{22}, (that is, the first subscript indicates whether the apparatus is the left- or right-hand apparatus, and the right subscript indicates the orientation of the apparatus). Let λ be a hidden variable which is deterministic in that each triple of values $\langle \lambda_i, E_{1j}, E_{2k} \rangle$ determines a pair of results for the left- and right-hand experiments. The theory is *local in the first sense* iff the right-hand experimental result is a function only of the hidden variable and the right-hand experimental arrangement $\langle \lambda_i, E_{2k} \rangle$. Likewise for the left-hand experimental result. The motivation, of course, is

19. J. S. Bell, "Introduction to the Hidden Variable Question," in d'Espagnat, ed., *Foundations of Quantum Mechanics* (New York: Academic Press, 1971); and J. F. Clauser and M. A. Horne, "Experimental Consequences of Objective Local Theories," *Physical Review D*, vol. 10, no. 2 (1974):526–32.

20. This is the sense used in the original Bell theorem, which applied to deterministic hidden variables theories. See J. S. Bell, "On the Einstein-Podolsky-Rosen Paradox," *Physics* (1965):195–200; E. Wigner, "On Hidden Variables and Quantum Mechanical Probabilities," *American Journal of Physics* 38 (1970):1005–09; and P. Eberhard, "Bell's Theorem without Hidden Variables," *Il Nuovo Cimento*, vol. 38B, no. 1 (1977):75–79.

that which experiment is performed on the left can be made to depend on factors outside the past light cone of the experiment on the right. The result is that the statistical predictions of the theory in question cannot agree with those of quantum mechanics.

The hidden variable, λ, in the foregoing account need not be the sort of thing we normally have in mind as a hidden variable. Its sole function is to serve as a foundation for a counterfactual: what experimental results would have ensued had a certain experiment (which in fact was not performed) been performed? If we believe, on whatever grounds, that such counterfactuals are always true or false, then we can take the set of true subjunctives of the form:

> If measurements E_{1j}, E_{2k} were performed, results
> R_{1l}, R_{2m} would ensue,

as constituting the hidden variable, λ, in the foregoing account. Since subjunctives obey modus ponens (If, if p were the case q would be and p is the case, then q is the case) the theory is deterministic. The assumption that these conditionals have a truth value can thus be thought of as constituting a kind of minimal deterministic hidden variable theory. It cannot be local in the first sense if it is to agree with quantum mechanics.

One might hope to be able to accept quantum mechanics, and still avoid embracing a nonlocal theory, by denying that there is any true deterministic hidden variable theory, even one this modest. Let me call this position "Copenhagen?".

But Bell's results have been generalized by Bell and by Clauser and Horne to stochastic hidden variable theories. Here a more general sense of locality is required, and the sense which is used in these proofs is natural, given the earlier discussions in this book. Here the locality assumption is that any statistical relevance between the results of left- and right-hand experiments disappears within the cells of the partition generated by the hidden variables (and the experimental arrangement):

> $Pr(R_{1l} \,\&\, R_{2m}$ given $\lambda \,\&\, E_{1j} \,\&\, E_{2k}) =$
> $Pr(R_{1l}$ given $\lambda \,\&\, \dot{E}_{1j}) \, Pr(R_{2m}$ given $\lambda \,\&\, E_{2k})^{21}$

---

21. Or, fixing the experimental arrangement, $Pr(R_{1l} \,\&\, R_{2m}$ given $\lambda) =$

A theory is *local in the second sense* if the value of the hidden variable screens off correlations between spacelike separated events in the manner indicated.

Stochastic hidden variable theories that are local in this second sense are also shown to be incompatible with the predictions of quantum mechanics. Now, just as a set of deterministic conditionals from experimental arrangements to outcomes can be thought of as a minimal deterministic hidden variables theory, a set of conditionals from experimental arrangements to *probabilities of outcomes* can be thought of as a minimal stochastic hidden variables theory. Since quantum mechanics itself, as it is usually interpreted, grounds such conditionals, there is a clear sense in which quantum mechanics itself is a nonlocal theory.

Let me explain the last claim a little more fully. Suppose that we don't believe in hidden variables in the usual sense. And suppose we take the "Copenhagen?" position that deterministic subjunctives from experimental arrangements to outcomes, in cases where that experiment is not performed, lack a truth value. Can we then say that the question of locality for quantum mechanics itself *simply doesn't arise*! I think not. The "Copenhagen?" position may render the question of locality in the first sense-ill defined, but the question of locality in the second sense remains.

There are still the subjunctives from experimental arrangements to *probabilities of outcomes*. A precise version on the statistical (Born) interpretation of quantum mechanics is that such conditonals always have a truth value, determined by the state vector. We can take the bundle of true conditionals of this form (or the state vector itself as in Eberhardt) as λ, and ask whether this λ screens off the correlation between spacelike separated outcomes. The answer is negative. In this sense, quantum mechanics itself is a nonlocal theory.

Consideration of the collapse of the wave packet in the Einstein-Podolsky-Rosen situation reveals some subtle

---

$Pr(R_{1l}$ given $\lambda) Pr(R_{2m}$ given $\lambda)$, as in Clauser and Horne, "Experimental Consequences of Objective Local Theories."

distinctions with regard to locality. (1) Locality is preserved in the sense that collapse of the wave packet *does
not allow the transfer of energy-momentum* between
spacelike separated events.[22] (2) We cannot use the collapse of the wave packet to *signal* between spacelike separated events because the probabilities of an outcome there,
given that a measurement was made here (but not given
the outcome of the measurement), remain the same. Since
I can only arrange that a measurement be made here, but
not its outcome, I cannot use the measuring process to
signal. Locality, in this sense, is preserved by the character of the resiliency of the quantum mechanical probabilities. (3) But in the sense of locality that requires that
correlation between spacelike separated events always be
factorable-out by a common cause, the sense coordinate
with the Mill-Edgeworth-Yule-Suppes-Cartwright treatment of causality of the last section, quantum mechanics
itself, and any hidden variable theory which reproduces
the quantum-mechanical probabilities, must be nonlocal.

---

22. Even this statement requires qualification in light of the uncertainty principle, not because it is ever false, but because its terms cannot
be simultaneously regarded as well defined to arbitrary levels of preci-
sion.

IIC The Role of Causal Factors in Rational Decision

There is a difference between inquiry and deliberation; for deliberation is inquiry into a particular kind of thing. . . .

. If, then, it is characteristic of men of practical wisdom to have deliberated well, excellence in deliberation will be correctness with regard to what conduces to the end of which practical wisdom is the true apprehension. (Ch. 9)

Practical wisdom, then, must be a reasoned and true state of capacity to act with regard to human goods. (Ch. 5)

It is to be noted that nothing that is past is an object of choice, e.g. that no one chooses to have sacked Troy; for no one deliberates about the past, but about the future and what is capable of being otherwise, while what is past is not capable of not having taken place; hence Agathon is right in saying:

> *For this alone is lacking even to God*
> *To make undone things that have once been done.*
>
> (Ch. 2)

Aristotle
Nicomachean Ethics

There is a class of decision situations which are prima facie counterexamples to the rule. "Choose that act which maximizes the expected utility conditional on that act."[1] These examples have a prima facie moral: that the concept of conditional expected utility does not give causal considerations their due weight in rational decision.

Suppose that the connection between hardening of the arteries and cholesterol intake turned out to be like this:

---

1. As in Jeffrey, *The Logic of Decision* (New York: McGraw-Hill, 1965). My understanding of these matters owes much to discussions with Nancy Cartwright, Richard Jeffrey, and David Lewis.

hardening of the arteries is not caused by cholesterol intake like the clogging of a water pipe; rather it is caused by a lesion in the artery wall. In an advanced state these lesions will catch cholesterol from the blood, a fact which has deceived previous researchers about the causal picture. Moreover, imagine that once someone develops the lesion he tends to increase his cholesterol intake. We do not know what mechanism accounts for this effect of the lesion. We do, however, know that the increased cholesterol intake is beneficial; it somehow slows the development of the lesion. Cholesterol intake among those who do not have the lesion appears to have no effect on vascular health. Given this (partly) fanciful account of the etiology of atherosclerosis, what would a rational man who believed the account do when made an offer of Eggs Benedict for breakfast? I say that he would accept. He would be a *fool* to try to "make it the case that he had not developed the lesion" by curtailing his cholesterol intake.

It appears, then, that he would be a fool to maximize conditional expected utility. Although he is quite sure that high cholesterol intake is not a *causative* factor in the etiology of atherosclerosis, he nevertheless quite properly assigns probabilities such that the probability of atherosclerosis *conditional on* high cholesterol intake is much higher than its probability conditional on low cholesterol intake. The epistemic conditional probabilities do not mirror the cause-effect relation, but this is a phenomenon with which we are already familiar. It appears, then, that the rule of maximizing conditional expected utility (i.e., the average utility of outcomes weighted by the probability of those outcomes conditional on the act) leads us to the conclusion that we should refrain from the Eggs Benedict even when we are in possession of causal information which tells us that this is a futile attempt to manipulate the cause by suppressing its symptoms.

Examples could be multiplied. R. A. Fisher once suggested that the correlation between smoking and lung cancer might be due to them both being effects of a common genetic cause. Fisher's hypothesis has not fared well, but if, contrary to the evidence, it were true and you knew it to be true, and smoking were consistently pleasurable and not harmful in other ways, you would be foolish to refrain from smoking in order to lower the probability of having the smoking-cancer gene. You either have it or not, and you can't influence your genetic makeup by abstinence. A crude caricature of Calvanism holds that it is already (in time) decided who are the elect and who are the damned. A sign of being one of the elect is leading a virtuous life, dissolute living being a mark of the damned. It is supposed to be, according to this story, an inducement to virtue that it raises the probability of being one of the elect. It is an odd utilitarian who would buy such an inducement, and who would not at least prefer rewards for virtue under an arrangement with a last judgment. The infamous Newcomb paradox is to the same effect:[2] There are two boxes, one transparent and one opaque. The transparent box contains a thousand dollars. The choice is either (1) to take only the contents of the opaque box or (2) to take the contents of both boxes. A very reliable predictor has already placed a million dollars under the opaque box if he predicted that the agent would choose (1), otherwise nothing. Should the agent choose only the opaque box in order to "make it more likely that the predictor so predicted and stashed the million," rather than taking everything that's there? Should one avoid going to the doctor to reduce the probability that one is seriously ill?

There is a defense for the conditional expected utility principle against such counterexamples—one which can be pushed very far, but not, I think, far enough.[3] Returning to our original example, *if* the lesions increased cholesterol intake by producing a certain phenomenologically identifiable tickle in the taste buds, and if our rational man knew this and noticed whether he had the tickle or not, then maximizing expected utility would do for him. We can plausibly assume that having the tickle (and, equally well, not having it) screens off the correlation be-

2. See R. Nozick, "Newcomb's Paradox and Two Principles of Choice," in N. Rescher, ed., *Essays in Honor of Carl G. Hempel* (Dordrecht: Reidel, 1969).

3. I have heard this defense independently from Frank Jackson, Richard Jeffrey, David Lewis, and Isaac Levi.

tween atherosclerosis and high cholesterol intake. That is, the probability of atherosclerosis conditional on a tickle that has been resisted is no lower than that conditional on a tickle that has been indulged. Likewise the cholesterol glutton unprompted by a tickle is just as unlikely to have the disease as the untickled abstainer. Tickled or not, the conditional expected utility maximizer may have his feast. With little effort one can concoct stories with the counterpart of the tickle for many other examples—a craving or loathing for tobacco in the Fisher example; an internal voice speaking for sin or saintliness for the pseudo-Calvinist; symptoms for the patient contemplating a medical examination—and there is no question that the counterpart of the tickle does the trick if it really is there. But why should it always be there? *Why should we, in every decision situation, be in possession of knowledge of some convenient factor which screens off any probabilistic relationship which does not mirror a causal relationship?* After all, there need not be a tickle. The mechanism responsible for the increased intake of cholesterol might operate in any number of ways, conscious or unconscious, and the agent making the decision might not have a clue as to how it operates. For him, the example retains its force.

But, it might be argued, if the agent is rational the increased intake of cholesterol must operate through his utilities, probabilities, and decision rule. His prior knowledge of *these* can then plausibly be held to screen off the correlation between cholesterol intake and hardening of the arteries. I find this medicine hard to swallow. If the utilities, probabilities, and decision rule determine the action, then it is tantamount to taking which action will be performed as a *datum* in the evaluation of the alternative courses of action. The whole decision process then threatens to become dangerously self-referential. This threat never materializes only because the whole decision process becomes ill defined. That is, if the probability of one of the alternative actions, A_1, is taken as equal one, then the probabilities conditional on its competitors, and thus their conditional expected utilities, are ill defined. Putting that problem aside for a moment, we see that perfect knowledge of the action to be chosen will screen off all right, but with a vengeance. If the probability of A_1 is one, then the probability of any consequence conditional on A_1 is equal to its unconditional probability, and thus the conditional expected utility of A_1 is equal to its unconditional expected utility. Correlations with causal consequences of the action are here screened off in just the same way as correlations with causal preconditions. We are trying to push the idea of the tickle too far, and the strain is showing. It would be better to search for a model of rational decision that would accommodate the tickle, but would not require it.

In 1975 Allan Gibbard and William Harper suggested a model in which the conditional probabilities are replaced by probabilities of subjunctives.[4] The Gibbard-Harper expectation of an act, A, over a set of possible outcomes, $\{O_j\}$, is: $\Sigma_j Pr$(If A were done then O_j) Value (O_j). Gibbard and Harper do not propose a theory of subjunctive conditionals, but rather rely on our untutored intuitions about subjunctives.[5] The latitude for interpretation that subjunctives allow makes this a kind of minimal theory, to the effect that there is a way of resolving the ambiguity of the subjunctive that gives the right answer.[6] So taken, the model permits an intuitive treatment of all the examples we have discussed.

One might hope, however, for something more definite, for a model that is not so subject to the ambiguity of subjunctive conditionals. I have the following suggestion. When we make a decision, some factors are outside the influence of our action.[7] (Without drawing too fine a line,

4. A. Gibbard and W. Harper, "Counterfactuals and Two Kinds of Expected Utility," Discussion Paper 194, Center for Mathematical Studies in Economics and Management Science, Northwestern University (Evanston, Illinois, 1975). Gibbard and Harper report that they were following a suggestion made by Robert Stalnaker in 1972.

5. They do, however, have a Stalnaker-type treatment in mind as a working hypothesis.

6. Note that this must be an interpretation which does not allow subjunctive conditionals from symptom to cause.

7. I do not deny that this notion may involve subjunctive judgments, but the problem is more sharply circumscribed if the judgments required are restricted in this way.

we can agree that in normal situations what has happened before the action is outside its influence. The mass of the sun tomorrow is also outside the influence of my actions today, etc.) I suggest that relative to each possible combination of the factors outside our influence, we calculate the conditional expected utility of our action, holding those factors fixed; and that we take the average of these expectations, weighting it by the probability that the factors are fixed in just that way. More precisely, let K_is be maximally specific specifications of the factors outside our influence at the time of decision which are causally relevant to the outcome of our actions, and let C_js be specifications of factors which may be influenced by our actions. Then I suggest that we should maximize the K-expectation:[8]

$$U_K(A) = \Sigma_i Pr(K_i) \, \Sigma_j Pr(C_j \text{ given } K_i \, \& \, A) \text{ Utility}$$
$$(C_j \, \& \, K_i \, \& \, A)$$
$$= \Sigma_{i,j} Pr(K_i)Pr(C_j \text{ given } K_i \, \& \, A) \text{ Utility}$$
$$(C_j \, \& \, K_i \, \& \, A)$$

If it be granted that the past is outside our influence, then given my medical fantasy about the role of cholesterol we should breakfast in style.

Notice that in the special case where the factors outside our influence are statistically independent of the action $(Pr(K_i) = Pr(K_i \text{ given } A))$, the K-expectation coincides with the Jeffrey-expected utility. So many ordinary cases of decision-making approximate this condition that one must go to some length to find counterexamples to the rule of maximizing conditional expected utility. Furthermore, notice that when everything is within our influence the K-expectation again collapses to *Jeffrey-expected utility* $(\Sigma_j Pr(C_j \text{ given } A) \, U(C_j \, \& \, A))$. On the other hand, if all the relevant factors are outside our control, the K-expectation collapses to *Savage-expected utility* $(\Sigma_i Pr(K_i)U \, (K_i \, \& \, A))$.[9]

8. I circulated a more complicated form of this proposal in spring 1977. The reduction of the suggested decision rule to this simpler, equivalent form is due to Richard Jeffrey and David Lewis.

9. Jeffrey-expected utility = conditional expected utility as in R. Jeffrey, *The Logic of Decision*. By Savage-expected utility I mean unconditional expected utility where the outcomes are chosen to be indepen-

Suppose that for every K_i the expectation relative to K_i ($\Sigma_j Pr(C_j$ given $K_i \& A) U(C_j \& K_i \& A)$) of an act, A, is greater than that of any competing act. Then act A is said to *dominate* its competitors relative to the partition $\{K_i\}$ generated by the factors outside our influence. If an act is dominant relative to $\{K_i\}$, then the rule of maximizing the K-expectation will tell us to choose it.[10]

An illuminating way to view the K-expectation is as a double expectation—as the subjective expectation of objective expected utility. The K-expectation is:

$$\Sigma_i PR(K_i)\, \Sigma_j PR(C_j \text{ given } K_i \& A)\, V(C_j \& K_i \& A)$$

(where PR is epistemic probability). Then let $pr_i(p)$ be the objectified probability $PR(p$ given $k_i)$: the probability conditional on the fixed factors being fixed in the i-th possible way. And let $v_i(p)$ be the objectified value $V(p \& K_i)$; the value that p would have together with a background of fixed factors fixed in the i-th possible way. Then the K-expectation may be rewritten as an epistemic expectation of an objectified expectation:

$$\Sigma_i PR(K_i)\, \Sigma_j pr_i(C_j \text{ given } A)\, v_i(C_j \& A)$$

The rule of maximizing expected utility has not been abandoned, but rather applied twice!

But it remains that we have different types of expectation at each level. The objectified expectation, $\Sigma_j pr_i(C_j$ given $A) v_i(C_j \& A)$, is *conditional* expected utility. Its epistemic expectation is *unconditional* ($PR(K_i)$ rather

dent, in some suitable sense, from the act. There are other elements of Savage's *framework* that I do not presuppose when I use his expected utility *formula*. In Savage's framework acts are not elements in the probability space, but rather functions from states of the world to payoffs. See L. J. Savage, *The Foundations of Statistics* (New York: Wiley, 1954). In Jeffrey, on the other hand, acts are represented as propositions, which are elements of the probability space. The K-expectation, then, requires a Jeffrey- rather than a Savage-type framework, and the discussion of this section is to be taken as proceeding within such a framework. Isaac Levi considers and rejects the application of what I call *Savage-expected utility* to Newcomb-type situations in "Newcomb's Many Problems," *Theory and Decision* 6 (1975):161–75, although he does not mention Savage explicitly.

10. Thus Nozick's intuitions about dominance are given their proper place. See R. Nozick, "Newcomb's Paradox and Two Principles of Choice." Compare Levi's discussion of Nozick in "Newcomb's Many Problems."

than $PR(K_i \text{ given } A)$).[11] This is just because the K_is have been chosen so that they are outside the influence of our actions.

A further question arises as to whether one's real preferences have a Jeffrey-representation. That is, can we find a fictitious probability-utility framework such that maximizing conditional expected utility in that framework gives the same result as maximizing the K-expectation in the real probability-utility framework? If this were possible we could always find a probability-utility representation in which causal factors were already discounted, and in which maximizing conditional expected utility was still king. I don't think that it is possible. It is, on the face of it, unlikely that such a result can be obtained, since what factors are outside the influence of our action will vary with the action in question. But *for a given action* and fixed division of the causally relevant factors into those outside and those inside our influence, such a fictitious probability-utility framework (and indeed one with the same utilities) *can always be found*, so that we can always save the appearance of maximizing conditional expected utility "locally," although not globally.

Here's how: Let Pr_f denote the fictitious distribution and $Pr_f(A_m) = Pr_i(A_m)$. Let $Pr_f(K_i \& A_m) = Pr_f(K_i)Pr_f(A_m)$. exhaustive set of alternative actions. Take $Pr_f(K_i) = Pr_i(K_i)$ and $Pr_f(A_m) = Pr_i(A_m)$. Let $Pr_f(K_i \& A_m) = Pr_f(K_i) \, Pr_f(A_m)$. Let $Pr_f(C_j \& K_i \& A_m) = Pr_f(K_i \& A_m) \, Pr_i(C_j \text{ given } K_i \& A_m)$. Then the expected utility of each A_m on the basis of the new probability distribution is equal to its K-expectation on the basis of the old distribution since:

1. $Pr_f(K_i \text{ given } A_m) = Pr_i(A_m)$ and
2. $Pr_f(C_j \text{ given } K_i \& A_m) = Pr_i(C_j \text{ given } K_i \& A_m)$

Notice, that what we have done to save Jeffrey expectation is to make our fictitious distribution, Pr_f, resemble a kind of objective distribution. By hypothesis, the K_is are outside the influence of our actions, and the fictitious distribution makes them statistically independent. If the K_is

11. Indeed, making the epistemic expectation *conditional* would modify the K-expectation in such a way that it would collapse to the Jeffrey expectation.

were, in some sense, objectively as probable as they subjectively seem, then the fictitious distribution would be an objective distribution, and we would have another illustration of the rule operative in the K-expectation: *Jeffrey expectation for objective probabilities, Savage expectation for subjective probabilities.*

The problem is that to use the Jeffrey expectation we must know the objective probabilities, and we may not know them. But for Savage, and equally for the K-expectation, we must also know something objective: we must know that the K_is are suitably independent of the act. What if we *don't know* which factors are outside our influence? The answer is that we can always construct various hypotheses about what is outside our influence, such that the truth values of these hypotheses are factors outside our influence.[12] Let the factors that are outside our sphere of influence according to H_n be the K_{ni}s, and those susceptible to our influence according to it be the C_{ni}s. Now the new factors outside our influence have the form $H_n \& K_{ni}$. The K-expectation then becomes:

$$\Sigma_{nij} Pr(H_n \& K_{ni}) Pr(C_{nj} \text{ given } H_n \& K_{ni} \& A) \, U(C_{nj} \& H_n \& K_{ni} \& A)[13]$$

In the simplest cases the hypotheses will be independent probabilistically and neutral with respect to utility in the following ways:

$$Pr(H_n \& K_{ni}) = Pr(H_n) Pr(K_{ni})$$
$$Pr(C_{nj} \text{ given } H_n \& K_{ni} \& A) = Pr(C_{nj} \text{ given } K_{ni} \& A)$$
$$U(C_{nj} \& H_n \& K_{ni} \& A) = U(C_{nj} \& K_{ni} \& A)$$

In these special cases we will get the same result as if we had on each hypothesis computed the K-expectation and

12. I learned the trick from David Lewis. It is originally due to Savage. See L. J. Savage, *The Foundations of Statistics*; D. Krantz et al., *Foundations of Measurement* (New York: Academic Press, 1971), vol. 1, ch. 8; and Jeffrey, "Savage's Omelet," in *PSA 1976* 2:361–71. Ellery Eells points out that which factors are outside the influence of my action may depend on the particular action in question, rather than just the set of alternative actions. This would require a slightly more complicated treatment, but one not different in principle.

13. Actually taking the new Cs to be the $H_m \& C_{mj}$, and plugging into the definition, we get $\Sigma_{nmij} Pr(H_n \& K_{ni}) Pr(H_m \& C_{mj} \text{ given } H_n \& K_{ni} \& A)$ $U(H_m \& C_{mj} \& H_n \& K_{ni} \& A)$, but the cross terms drop out since $Pr(H_m \& C_{mj} \text{ given } H_n \& K_{ni} \& A) = 0$ when $n \neq m$).

then taken the probability-weighted average of the results. Incorporating the H_ns into the factors, however, allows the model to deal with even more complex samples where the hypotheses are relevant both to the probabilities and to the utilities.

An example may serve to suggest the complexities that can be handled in this way. Someone is deciding whether or not to smoke, and is worried about lung cancer. He assigns some positive probability to each of the following hypotheses:

Hypothesis 1.

> *Fatalism:* Whether he gets cancer or not is already decided by the gods and is outside the influence of his action. Either
>
> K_{11} the gods have decided he will get cancer or
> K_{12} they have decided that he won't.

Hypothesis 2.

> *Fisher:* Smoking and cancer are effects of a (probabilistic) genetic common cause.
>
> K_{21} he has the gene
> K_{22} he doesn't.

Hypothesis 3.

> *Multiple causation:* Genetic factors, early environmental exposure to pollutants, and smoking are all contributing probabilistic causes of cancer. A precancerous condition, *carcinoma in situ,* is a probabilistic cause of smoking. Genetic factors, early exposure to pollutants, and the existence at the time of decision of *carcinoma in situ* are all factors outside the influence of the act. The K_{3i}s are then all possible combinations of these factors.

Hypothesis 4.

> *Backward causation:* Cancer is genetically determined, but the decision to smoke or not can influence what genes one was born with. (A bizarre hypothesis, but this man may be a philosopher.) No factors are beyond his influence.

He may also, for moral reasons, attach more disutility to getting cancer if hypothesis (3) or (4) is true than if hypothesis (1) or (2) is. The skeptical reader may verify for

himself that all the twists of this example are given their
due weight in the suggested model of rational decision.

What, then, is the connection between the
K-expectation and the sort of approach suggested by Gibbard and Harper? Consider counterfactuals with (objectified) probabilistic consequents, of the form:

If A were the case then $pr(C_j)$ would be x

Suppose that where K_i is true, we take the value of x
which makes the foregoing conditional true to be the objectified probability of C_j given A:

$x = pr_i(C_j \text{ given } A) = PR(C_j \text{ given } A \ \& \ K_i)$

Suppose that we further assume that the values with
which we are dealing are invariant over the K_is, that is:

$V(p) = V(p \ \& \ K_i)$

Then the K-expectation is equivalent to:

$\Sigma_{x,j} x \, PR(\text{If } A \text{ were the case,}$

then $pr(C_j)$ would be x) $V(C_j \ \& \ A)$

which is a form of "Gibbard-Harper decision theory with
chancy outcomes."[14]

Considerations of physics might convince us that, if
counterfactuals have truth values, almost the only true
counterfactuals are ones with probabilistic consequents.
Yet even those who know physics assert counterfactuals
that are not so qualified. I suggested, in section IIA4, that
we take as the basic assertibility value (BAV) of a subjunctive conditional with unqualified consequent, the epistemic expectation of the prior propensity of the consequent conditional on the antecedent. This is, in the case
at hand:

$BAV \ (\text{If } A \text{ were taken then } C_j \text{ would ensue})$
$= \Sigma_i PR(K_i) \, PR(C_j \text{ given } K_i \ \& \ A)$ [15]

14. Discussed in private correspondence between David Lewis and
Alan Gibbard in 1977 and in Lewis's paper "Chancy Causation," read at
the Pittsburgh Conditional Expected Utility Conference, November
1978.

15. Given the assumptions regarding conditionals with chancy consequents which were used in the last paragraph to reduce "Gibbard-
Harper decision theory with chancy outcomes" to the K-expectation,
notice that, for the conditionals involved here, BAV (If p were, then q) =
$\Sigma_x x \, PR(\text{If } p \text{ were, then } pr(q) = x)$. The idea of using this sort of identification to reduce the counterfactual decision theory with chancy con-
sequents to that with unqualified consequents is suggested by Alan Gibbard in correspondence in 1977.

On the assumption that this suggestion is correct, and re-
taining the qualification that the values are independent
of the K_is, we can rewrite the K-expectation as:

$\Sigma_j BAV$(If A were taken,

then C_j would ensue) $V(C_j \& A)$

which casts it in the form of the original Gibbard-Harper
suggestion.[16]

I can therefore accept both Gibbard-Harper decision
theory and Lewis's generalization thereof to conditionals
with chancy consequents, for given my analysis of the
subjunctives involved both collapse to the K-expectation. I
must accept Savage's *formula* for the expectation to be
maximized:

$\Sigma_i PR(K_i) V(K_i \& A)$

for the expectation is of that form, with $V(K_i \& A)$ being
further analyzed as $\Sigma_j PR(C_j$ given $K_i \& A) V(C_j \& K_i \& A)$.
That further analysis, however, is not open to Savage, for
$PR(C_j$ given $K_i \& A)$ is not even well defined within his
framework. What is required for the further analysis is
that we move from a Savage framework to a Jeffrey
framework, within which the suggested analysis of $V(K_i \&$
$A)$ is possible. The challenge of the Newcomb examples
and of suggestions of Stalnaker-Gibbard-Harper-Lewis
decision theory may not be as radical as they at first appear. A blend of the Jeffrey and Savage approaches in the
form of the K-expectation accommodates the examples in
a way consistent with the proposed subjunctive decision
rules.

16. There is a less reductionistic way to make the connection with
Gibbard-Harper, which was suggested to me by David Lewis, and that is
to frame the hypotheses, H_n, in the Savage trick in terms of subjunctives
with probabilistic consequents. My tastes here, however, are thoroughly
reductionistic, and I wish to avoid unanalyzed counterfactual machinery
as much as possible.

IID Scientific Explanation

No matter how long or carefully I observe the hands of my watch, the valves and wheels of a locomotive, or the buds of an oak, I know that I will not discover what makes bells chime, locomotives move, or spring breezes blow. To learn these things I must shift my viewpoint and study the laws which govern these things.

Leo Tolstoy
War and Peace

The notion of a good scientific explanation is far from precise. A good explanation will show the way from puzzlement to understanding; but the appropriate type of explanation will depend on the nature of the puzzlement. Still, we can say this: insofar as scientific understanding is codified in laws and theories, scientific explanation should consist in showing, in some way, how the item to be explained fits into the scientific nomological network. But exactly how explanatory accounts should do this is a question to which I can see no general answer. I will attempt something more modest: to distinguish several dimensions of "goodness" of scientific explanation which are to some extent independent. I do not claim that these are the only dimensions of "goodness," nor do I claim that there is or ought to be an aggregation function which combines goodness in various dimensions to give a unique sense of goodness overall.

I will be interested in explanations having a certain canonical form. Let us assume that what is to be explained is that a certain system is in a certain physical state S^*. Let $\{S_i\}$ be an exhaustive set of mutually exclusive *possible states of the system* of which S^* is a member. (Where the system is capable of an infinite number of alternative states, we assume some natural finite partition.) Let us also suppose that we have a set $\{E_j\}$ of *competing explanatory accounts* for the system's being in State S^*. (I do not assume that these accounts are mutually exclusive or exhaustive.) I also assume that for each account $\{E_j\}$ and each possible state $\{S_i\}$, we have the conditional probability of the account on the state, $Pr(S_i$ given $E_j)$. (It will be useful to assume that the set of explanatory accounts always contains a *null explanatory account*, E_{null} (a tautology will do): $Pr(S_i$ given $E_{null}) = Pr(S_i)$.) These conditional probabilities are not current epistemic probabilities. We don't try to *explain* a system's being in a state unless we know that it is in that state. Rather, we are interested in the prior objective conditional probabilities.

The first desideratum for an explanatory account is *truth*. The second desideratum is that the *connection between the explanatory account and the explanandum be lawlike*. In terms of the explication of lawlikeness offered in part I of this book, this comes to the requirement that the objective probability $Pr(S^*$ given $E_j)$ be highly resilient. Some trade-off is possible between these two desiderata. One can assure that $Pr(S^*$ given $E_j)$ is resilient by including in E_j some statement of propensity so construed as to require for its confirmation the resiliency in question.[1]

The third desideratum of an explanatory account is *explanatory power*, the degree to which an explanatory account renders the state to be explained more likely than other alternative states. An explanatory account might render S^* overwhelmingly likely, in the most favorable case; or it might render S^* more likely than all of the alternatives taken together, that is, more likely than not; or it might render S^* more likely than each of its competitors; and so forth. Degrees of explanatory power are relevant to the force with which the explanation resolves the puzzlement: why S^* rather than something else? The fourth desideratum of an explanatory account is *comparative strength*, the degree to which the explanatory account renders the explanandum more probable than do competing explanatory accounts. If $Pr(S^*$ given $E_i) > Pr(S^*$ given $E_j)$, then I shall say that E_i is a stronger explanation

1. See P. Railton, "A Deductive-Nomological Model of Scientific Explanation," *Philosophy of Science* 45 (1978):206–26.

of S^* than E_j. In the degenerate case where the only competitor for an explanatory account is the null explanation, the demand for comparative strength reduces to the demand for *positive statistical relevance* (i.e., that $Pr(S^*$ given $E) > Pr(S^*)$. It is noted in Rescher and Skyrms that, although closely related, explanatory power and comparative strength need not coincide in their ordering of explanatory accounts.[2] For example:

	E_1	E_2
S_1	0.0	0.1
S_2^*	0.4	0.3
S_3	0.6	0.2
S_4	0.0	0.2
S_5	0.0	0.2

E_1 has more comparative strength than E_2, but E_2 has more explanatory power in that it renders S_2^* more probable than any alternative state.

Hempel's pioneering studies in statistical explanation required (1) truth of the explanatory account and focused mainly on (3) explanatory power, and thus they stressed symmetry of explanation and prediction. Scriven's famous paresis example focused attention on positive statistical relevance, which we can see as a special case of (4) comparative strength:

> We can explain but not predict whenever we have a proposition of the form 'the only cause of X is A.' (I) For example, 'the only cause of paresis is syphilis.' Notice that this is perfectly compatible with the statement that A is often followed by X; in fact, very few syphilitics develop paresis. (II) Hence, when A is observed, we can predict that X is *more* likely to occur than without A, but still extremely unlikely. So, we must, on the evidence, still predict that it will *not* occur. But if it does, we can still appear to (I) provide and guarantee our explanation. . . . Hence an event that cannot be predicted from a certain set of well-

2. N. Rescher and B. Skyrms, "A Methodological Problem in the Evaluation of Explanations," *Nous* (May, 1968):121–29.

confirmed propositions can, if it occurs, be explained
by appeal to them.[3]

The importance of statistical relevance for explanation
has also often been stressed by Salmon. Jeffrey, on the
other hand, and following him Railton, stress the importance of (2) the lawlike nature of the conditional probabilities involved, and they argue that one may have an
acceptable scientific explanation even in the absence of
comparative strength and explanatory power.[4]

These four criteria for good scientific explanation are
stated in terms of truth and objective probability. If we are
uncertain as to the truth of the eligible explanatory accounts, or as to the correct objective probabilities, we can
do no better than evaluate explanatory accounts by the
epistemic expectations of objective desiderata. Note that
the prior propensity theory of subjunctives that I have advocated links the second and third considerations together with the requirement of high basic assertibility
value of the subjunctive: "If the explanatory account were
true, then the explanadum would be." If we add the first
consideration, we come to the conclusion that we have an
explanation that is good in the first three ways if we have
high basic assertibility value for the premises of a subjunctive modus ponens argument:

> If E were true, S would be
> But E is true
> Therefore S is

The fourth consideration ties in with the implicature of relevance of the antecedent to the consequent in the foregoing subjunctive. Explanatory accounts which correspond

3. M. Scriven, "Explanation and Prediction in Evolutionary
Theory," *Science* 130 (1959).
4. See, for instance, W. Salmon, "Statistical Explanation," in Col-
odny, ed., *Nature and Function of Scientific Theories* (Pittsburgh: Uni-
versity of Pittsburgh Press, 1970), pp. 173–231. R. Jeffrey, "Statistical
Explanation vs Statistical Inference," in N. Rescher, ed., *Essays in
Honor of Carl G. Hempel* (Dordrecht: Reidel, 1969), pp. 104–13, re-
printed in W. Salmon, *Statistical Explanation and Statistical Relevance*
(Pittsburgh: University of Pittsburgh Press, 1971), pp. 19–28. P. Railton,
" A Deductive-Nomological Model of Scientific Explanation."

to subjunctives wherein that implicature must be canceled fare poorly as explanations. The sun will rise tomorrow even if I try to stop it by psychokinesis, but my trying to stop it is no explanation of its rising. Another way to view these requirements of relevance is in the context of the statistical analysis of causation, wherein they are not mere implicatures. Thus we can see that all four considerations are respected when we have warrant for asserting: E and E causes S.

Let me illustrate the interplay of epistemic and objective probability distributions with a fictitious example. A historian wishes to explain the death of Molly Malone. It is fairly clear from the historical accounts that she had a fever, but not clear what kind of fever. Suppose that there are two kinds of fever compatible with the description and that, on the evidence, they are about equally probable. Both are virulent, but not equally so. Examining mortality statistics for Dublin at the time, making plausible assumptions about Molly's age, economic bracket, and general health, yields a chance of death given fever 1 of about 80 percent, with the figure rising to 92 percent for fever 2. The probability of death given fever is not very resilient in the epistemic distribution, but is more resilient in the two "objective" distributions corresponding to fever 1 and fever 2 respectively. Thus, in each of the objective distributions, fever can be taken as a good explanation of her death, so in our position of epistemic uncertainty about the correct objective distribution we can still judge it to be a good explanation.

The example could be complicated. Suppose there is some third fever which is hardly ever fatal and which has some very small chance of being the one Molly had. Then although the explanatory power of the fever explanation may be low in the "objective" distribution corresponding to fever 3, the low epistemic probability of fever 3 still allows for a high expectation of explanatory power.

Those who like cleaner examples and purer resiliency can construct a quantum analogue. The point is that we don't look for resiliency, explanatory power, and so forth, in the epistemic distribution but in the appropriate objective distributions, and then weight those evaluations by the epistemic probabilities of the corresponding objective distributions.

If goodness of explanation is multidimensional, we might ask in what sense of goodness, if any, is induction inference to the best explanation. One sense of goodness of an explanatory account is (1) the probability that it is true, so the slogan applies here, albeit in a trivial and uninteresting manner. As many people have noticed, a deeper sense in which it rings true can be extracted from Bayes' Theorem. Consider two incompatible explanatory accounts, E_j and E_k.

$$Pr(E_j \text{ given } S^*)/Pr(E_k \text{ given } S^*)$$
$$= [Pr(S^* \text{ given } E_j/Pr(S^* \text{ given } E_k)] \cdot [Pr(E_j)/Pr(E_k)]$$

Which explanatory account is more probable on the basis of the explanandum goes by (a) a priori probability of the explanatory account and (b) comparative strength. In the numerical example given where explanatory power disagrees with comparative strength, if we give the two explanatory accounts equal a priori probability, then the account which is more probable given the explanandum is E_1, the account with greater comparative strength. Considerations of resiliency and lawlikeness appear to play no part in determining the probability of an explanatory account, given the explanandum, although they may play a role in determining whether a true, probable explanatory account may be further dignified as *knowledge*.

IIE Knowledge

It is clear that knowledge is a subclass of true beliefs. . . . There is the man who looks at a clock when it is not going, though he thinks that it is, and who happens to look at it at the moment when it is right; this man acquires a true belief as to the time of day, but cannot be said to have knowledge. There is the man who believes, truly, that the last name of the prime minister in 1906 began with a B, but who believes this because he thinks that Balfour was prime minister then, whereas in fact it was Campbell Bannerman. There is the lucky optimist who, having bought a ticket for a lottery, has an unshakable conviction that he will win, and being lucky, does win. Such instances can be multiplied indefinitely, and show that you cannot claim to have known merely because you turned out right.

What character in addition to truth must a belief have in order to count as knowledge? The plain man would say that there must be sound evidence to support the belief.

Bertrand Russell
Human Knowledge, Its Scope and Limits

We suppose ourselves to have unqualified scientific knowledge of a thing, as opposed to knowing it in the accidental way in which the sophist knows, when we think we know the cause on which the fact depends.

Aristotle
Prior Analytics

The premises of demonstrated knowledge must be true, primary, immediate, better known, and primary to the conclusion, which is further related to them as effect to cause.

Aristotle
Prior Analytics

I have always said that belief was knowledge if it was (i) true, (ii) certain, and (iii) obtained by a reliable process. But the word 'process' is very unsatisfactory.

F. P. Ramsey, "Knowledge"
The Foundations of Mathematics

That knowledge is something over and above true belief is an insight we have from the founding fathers, but just what more is required to still a matter of lively dispute. What I wish to point out in this chapter is that there is more unity behind the various suggestions in the literature than might be apparent on the surface.

There has always been a tension between first- and third-person epistemology. The first-person epistemologist seeks maxims he can follow, given his situation, to attain knowledge; the third-person epistemologist seeks standards for external evaluation. In the formula "Knowledge is true belief plus X," the tension is already present, with *belief* representing the first-person perspective and *truth* representing the third-person perspective. Even at this level some tussling has gone on, with, on the one hand, attempts to replace truth with warranted assertibility or to redefine it as coherence; and, on the other hand, attempts to construe belief behavioristically. When it comes to the X, the first-person point of view locates the missing factor in some sort of *rational warrant or justification*. Rational justification is usually taken to be some combination of good evidence (Russell's "plain man") and good inference (Aristotle's scientific syllogism), although the regress generated must always ultimately raise the question as to whether some beliefs must not have noninferential warrant either by virtue of some special status with respect to either the senses or intuition, or in accordance with some coherence theory of warrant. The third-person approach to the missing factor is exemplified by Ramsey's emphasis on *reliability* and by related requirements of a nomic or causal connection between the object of knowledge and the belief in question.

Russell's lucky optimist who wins the lottery lacks the internal factor of rational warrant or justification, and so fails to have knowledge. Russell's man who looks at the clock that is not going may, however, with suitable embroidery on the story, have perfectly good rational warrant for believing that the clock is telling him the right time—as good as we have for believing most things we call knowledge—and yet he fails to have knowledge.[1] Here the reliability of the process—the requisite lawlike or causal connection—fails for reasons external to the epistemic agent. Both internal and external constraints are necessary.

But first-person constraints can be assimilated to third-person ones. We certainly think that forming beliefs in a rationally warranted way is a more reliable way of forming true beliefs than relying on blind prejudice, whim, and so forth; and if we did not think so, we would change our conception of rationally warranted belief.

Let us focus, then, on the requirements of reliability, or causal or nomic connection. The causal requirement, if interpreted as something over and above the requirement of nomic connection, is incorrect, as is shown by the example of the man with the severed head. A man is seen lying in the gutter with his head severed, and is thereby known to be dead. Yet the severing of the head is not the cause of death, nor did the death cause the severing of the head. It is enough that the severed head is nomically sufficient (*ceteris paribus*) for death. We are left with nomic versus

---

1. The case of a normally trustworthy witness, who, for extraordinary reasons unknown to the subject, is determined to report a falsehood in this case, and yet blunders into telling the truth, is no different in principle.

reliability conditions, but it should be clear by now that I think that these come to much the same thing.[2]

What do we mean when we say that an instrument is *reliable*? We mean that it will give appropriate results, if its conditions of applicability are met, under a wide variety of circumstances. A reliable clock is one that keeps good time, given that it is set properly, wound regularly, and so forth. Of course, the reliability is never absolute, but only over some variety of circumstances normally encountered. The reliability of the instrument may be *defeated* by other circumstances, such as an intense magnetic field, which alter the relevant objective probabilities. What I am saying is that reliability is a *propensity* to produce correct results given the conditions of application of the instrument. By the lights of the theory of laws put forward in this book, nomic and reliability accounts of knowledge come to the same thing. Conversely, one might say that the theory of laws put forward here is a *reliability theory of laws*: laws are well confirmed when the probabilities are such as to vouchsafe their reliability as inferential instruments.

Let us apply these ideas to the reliability of the inferences the epistemic subject makes. Deductively valid and (hopefully) inductively strong arguments are reliable instruments for indicating true conclusions, given that they are supplied with true premises. But a false premise breaks the reliability of the process just as a mainspring that cracks from metal fatigue breaks the reliability of a watch. For these reasons, Ramsey proposed what has come to be known as a defeasibility account *as a consequence of the reliability theory.* He writes:

> We might then say, a belief obtained by a reliable process must be caused by what are not beliefs in a way or with accompaniments that can be more or less relied on to give true beliefs, and if in this train of causation

2. As do Ramsey and Armstrong. See F. P. Ramsey, *The Foundations of Mathematics and Other Logical Essays* (London: Routledge & Kegan Paul, 1931), and D. Armstrong, *Belief, Truth and Knowledge* (London: Cambridge University Press, 1973).

occur other intermediary beliefs, these must all be true ones.[3]

Ramsey's requirement comes to something more than requiring that the overall process, considered as a black box, be reliable. It comes to requiring that its subprocesses be reliable as well. Thus Ramsey says: "Perhaps we should not say (iii) obtained by a reliable process, but (iii) formed in a reliable way." It should be clear, however, that this additional constraint is not restricted to the inferences of the epistemic agent. If I have a chain of instruments, two of which fail in compensating ways—or if Tom lies to Harry, and Harry attempts to lie to me but inadvertently tells the truth—then I do not have in these a sufficient basis for knowledge. The external failure of reliability may come at some level about which I have no theory and thus no false belief.[4] Thus the reliability account is more general than the defeasibility account alone.

This application of the reliability theory to internal reasoning explains Russell's third example—the progenitor of the Gettier examples—the man who correctly believes that the last name of the prime minister in 1906 began with a B on the basis of the incorrect belief that he was Balfour.

To the extent to which resiliency is important both for knowledge and for good explanation, we have further backing for Harman's idea that knowledge is inference to the best explanation. Resiliency of the probability of the explanandum given the explanatory account can contribute to resiliency of the explanatory account given the explanandum (although it does not guarantee it) via Bayes's theorem:

$$Pr(K \text{ given } E \& F_i) = [Pr(E \text{ given } K \& F_i) \cdot Pr(K \text{ given } F_i)]/Pr(E \text{ given } F_i)$$

How far should reliability or resiliency be pushed before we have knowledge? Not to an absolute requirement

3. F. P. Ramsey, "Knowledge," in *The Foundations of Mathematics and Other Essays.*
4. Of course, the right kind of philosopher may have some general covering belief about reliability which fails, but having the right theory of knowledge is hardly a prerequisite for knowledge.

of universal scope, if we wish to retain some descriptive use for the word. (This is what the standard skeptical arguments teach us.) How far then? Here I think we approach the point where fine tuning leads to rapidly diminishing returns, and where we should take to heart Russell's remark: "Let us remember that the question 'What do we mean by 'knowledge'?' is not one to which there is a definite and unambiguous answer, any more than to the question 'What do we mean by 'baldness'?' "

IIF* Resiliency and Rules of Acceptance

In actual practice, people do not carry around probability assignments in (0,1) for every contingent proposition; at a certain point they simply *accept* a proposition and in some sense treat it as a datum. Some epistemologists have sought a rational reconstruction of this process in an idealized setting by looking for rules of acceptance or detachment which would be keyed to the structure of the relevant probabilities. Carnap and others have argued against the feasibility of such a reconstruction on the grounds that any such rule would throw away probabilistic information which would be crucial in some decision-theoretic context. Carnap's objection is well taken, but it is only decisive within the context of a model where it costs nothing to store such information. Since no one, except perhaps God, is in this happy state, it is still of interest to investigate the properties of various rules of acceptance.

Let us call a rule of acceptance *strongly consistent* iff for any probability distribution the set of statements it leads one to accept is consistent. Strong consistency is an attractive property for a rule of acceptance to have, but the example of the lottery shows how difficult it is to come by. Consider the following propositions concerning a fair lottery: P_0—one of the tickets from 1 to n will win; P_1—ticket 1 won't win; P_2—ticket 2 won't win; . . . P_n—ticket n won't win.

A requirement of high probability alone will not yield a strongly consistent rule of acceptance. For by choosing an n sufficiently large, we can plausibly make each proposition in the series P_0 . . . P_n as probable as you please, although the propositions are, taken as a whole, inconsistent. Indeed, if our probability function is real-valued, an infinite lottery (we may think of a denumerably infinite lottery, or a nondenumerable one, e.g., the point dart thrown at the unit interval) yields an example where each P_n has probability 1 and yet the set of P_ns is inconsistent. If we go to a nonarchimedean-valued measure to preserve strict coherence, as I suggested in the section on infinite probability spaces (IC1), then probability 1 will be reserved for logical truths; but the infinite lottery paradox yields an example of an inconsistent set of sentences, each of whose members has a probability infinitesimally close to 1.

What high probability cannot do, high resiliency can, at least if resiliency is taken in the strongest sense. In the following discussion, we take resiliency as resiliency over the language, as defined in the section on infinite probability spaces, and assume strict coherence of the probability measure. The requirements of this sort of resiliency are strong indeed:

Theorem:

> The set of statements, S, with resiliency greater than .5 over the language forms a chain with respect to logical implication.

Proof:

> Assume the contrary, that S contains two sentences, p_i, p_j, such that neither entails the other. Then let $p_i{}^* = p_i \mathrel{\&} \sim p_j$ and $p_j{}^* = \sim p_i \mathrel{\&} p_j$. $p_i{}^*$ and $p_j{}^*$ are both self-consistent but they are mutually incompatible. Then $R_L(p_i) \leqslant Pr(p_i{}^*$ given $p_i{}^* \mathrel{\lor} p_j{}^*) = Pr(p_i{}^*)/Pr(p_i{}^*) + Pr(p_j{}^*)$ and $R_L(p_j) \leqslant Pr(p_j{}^*$ given $p_i{}^* \mathrel{\lor} p_j{}^*) = Pr(p_j{}^*)/(Pr(p_i{}^*) + Pr(p_j{}^*))$. So either $Pr(p_i{}^*) \leqslant Pr(p_j{}^*)$, in which case $R_L(p_i) \leqslant 1/2$; or not, in which case $R_L(p_j) \leqslant 1/2$.

Corollary 1:

> If L is a first-order language, the set of propositions of L with resiliency greater than .5 is consistent.

Proof:

> Each member of the set is consistent, since it has resiliency greater than .5. Each finite subset of the set is consistent, for it is a chain with respect to logical implication. So for each finite subset there is a consistent proposition in the chain that implies every member of the chain. The set is consistent by compactness.

We may, however, also be interested in incompact languages.

Corollary 2:

Let L be a denumerable language and let the propositions of L form a sigma algebra (closure under denumerable conjunctions and disjunctions), and let Pr be a sigma-additive regular measure on it. Then the set of propositions of L with resiliency greater than .5 is consistent.

Proof:

Each proposition of S has probability greater than .5 and S is a chain with respect to implication. Then, by sigma additivity, the probability of the denumerable conjunction of the members of S is greater than .5.

Appendix 1
Probability Refresher

Probabilities are numerical values assigned to elements of some Boolean algebra. Here we may think of the Boolean algebra as composed of a set of sentences or propositions such that conjunctions, disjunctions, and negations of sentences in the set are also in it. These numerical values must satisfy three simple rules:

1. Probability values must be greater than or equal to zero.
2. The probability of a tautology is equal to one.
3. Probability values are additive; that is, if the conjunction of p with q is a contradiction, then the probability of their disjunction, $p \lor q$, is the sum of the probabilities of the disjuncts.

(It is mathematically convenient to add the further condition of total additivity, or Σ-additivity, which requires that the probability of an infinite disjunction of incompatible disjuncts be equal to the limit of the sequence of partial sums of probabilities of elements of the sequence of disjuncts. We will not make this further assumption, because there seems no good philosophical reason to believe that probabilities are always totally additive. Total additivity is not required for coherence of degrees of belief. At the other end of the spectrum, relative frequencies need not be totally additive. We will think of total additivity as a special case rather than as part of the definition of probability.[1])

From these simple rules we can derive, for example:

The probability of a contradiction is 0.
Probability values are less than or equal to 1.
$Pr(\sim p) = 1 - Pr(p)$
$Pr(p \lor q) = Pr(p) + Pr(q) - Pr(p \lor q)$
$Pr(p) = Pr(p \,\&\, q) + Pr(p \,\&\, \sim q)$
etc.

1. See B. De Finetti, *Theory of Probability* (New York: Wiley, 1970), vol. 1, pp. 116–33; vol. 2, pp. 348–61; and T. Fine, *Theories of Probability* (New York: Academic Press, 1973), pp. 67–68.

If, in addition, a probability distribution awards probability 1 only to tautologies (and thus probability 0 only to contradictions), it is said to be *regular*. (There is a philosophical reason why at least epistemic probabilities should be regular; strict coherence of degrees of belief entails regularity.[2]) We will assume in this book, unless otherwise stated, that epistemic probabilities are regular. (For technical reasons, this sometimes requires introduction of infinitesimal probabilities, a matter which is reserved for appendix 4.)

The *conditional probability* of q on p, $Pr(q$ given $p)$, is equal, by definition, to $Pr(p \& q)/Pr(p)$ when $Pr(p) \neq 0$. Regularity has the pleasant consequence that the conditional probability is always defined, except where the condition is a contradiction. The definition of conditional probability has the immediate consequence that:

$$Pr(p \& q) = Pr(p) Pr(q \text{ given } p) = Pr(q) Pr(p \text{ given } q)$$

p and q are said to be *probabilistically* (statistically, stochastically) *independent* when $Pr(p \& q) = Pr(p) Pr(q)$, or, equivalently, when $Pr(q) = Pr(q$ given $p)$ or, equivalently, when $Pr(p) = Pr(p$ given $q)$. It is an immediate consequence of the definition of conditional probability that we have the *Bayes theorem:*

$$Pr(q \text{ given } p) = Pr(p \text{ given } q) Pr(q)/Pr(p) \text{ when}$$
$$Pr(p) \neq 0, Pr(q) \neq 0.$$

The probability-weighted average of some quantity is called its *expectation* or *expected value* (e.g., if George weighs either 100 or 200 pounds, with probabilities respectively of 1/3 and 2/3, then the expected value of George's weight is 1/3(100 lbs.) + 2/3(200 lbs.) = 166 2/3 lbs.).

A probability distribution, Pr_2, is said to come from another, Pr_1, *by conditionalization on a proposition, p,* if for every proposition, q, its new probability, $Pr_2(q)$, is equal to its old probability conditional on p, $Pr_1(q$ given $p)$.

A probability distribution, PR, is said to be a *mixture*

of other distributions, $pr_1, pr_2 \ldots pr_n$, if it is a weighted average of them, that is to say, if there are numbers, $w_1, w_2 \ldots w_n$, such that for every proposition, q, $PR(q) = [w_1 pr_1(q) + w_2 pr_2(q) + \ldots + w_n pr_n(q)]/w_1 + w_2 + \ldots + w_n$.

If the numerical weights operative in a mixture can in some sense be thought of as *probabilities* of the corresponding probability distributions, then the *mixture* can be thought of as an *expectation* of probability. For example, I think that a coin about to be flipped is either fair, F; or biased two-to-one in favor of heads, BH; or equally biased in favor of tails, BT. If BH, then the "objective" probability of heads is 2/3; if F, 1/2; if BT, 1/3. Suppose that my epistemic probability that the coin is fair is 1/3; likewise for the other two hypotheses about "objective" probability. Then it might be reasonable to take my epistemic probability as the weighted average of the "objective" probabilities, with the weights being the epistemic probabilities of those being the "right" objective probabilities:

$$PR_{epistemic}(heads) = PR_{epistemic}(BH)\, pr_{BH}(heads) +$$
$$PR_{epistemic}(F)\, pr_F(heads) +$$
$$PR_{epistemic}(BT)\, pr_{BT}(heads)$$
$$= 1/3\ 2/3 + 1/3\ 1/2 + 1/3\ 1/3 = 1/2$$

Here epistemic probability is the expectation of "objective" probability.

In an important sense, *conditionalization is an inverse of mixing*. This can be illustrated with reference to the foregoing example. If the coin is fair, then we can think of the "objective" probability of fairness as 1, $pr_F(F) = 1$, and the "objective" probability of heads and fairness as 1/2, $pr_F(F\ \&\ H) = pr_F(H) = 1/2$. Then, by definition, the "objective" conditional probability of heads given fairness comes out reasonably as 1/2, $pr_F(H\ given\ F) = pr_F(H) = 1/2$. Likewise, $pr_{BH}(H\ given\ BH) = pr_{BH}(H) = 2/3$, and $pr_{BT}(H\ given\ BT) = pr_{BT}(H) = 1/3$. If we take the epistemic distribution as the expectation of the "objective" distributions as above, we find that *these* conditional probabilities—the probabilities conditional on being in a certain "objective" distribution—remain the same in the epistemic distribution. E.g., $PR_e(F) = 1/3(1); PR_e(F\ \&\ H) = 1/3(1/2); PR_e(H\ given\ F) = 1/2 = pr_F(H\ given\ F) = pr_F(H)$. This means that we can recover the "objective" distribu-

tions from the epistemic distribution by conditionalizing
out: For any Q:

$$pr_F(Q) = PR_e(Q \text{ given } F)$$
$$pr_{BH}(Q) = PR_e(Q \text{ given } BH)$$
$$pr_{BT}(Q) = PR_e(Q \text{ given } BT)$$

If propositions characteristic of the elements of the mixture in the manner indicated for F, BH, BT are present in
the domain of the mixture, then conditionalizing out on
them accomplishes a separation of the mixture into its
original components.

In the foregoing example certain special conditional
probabilities remained the same in the mixture as in its
elements. It is important to bear in mind that this is *not*
typical. Suppose we modify the example to include two
flips of the coin and make the flips independent in each
"objective" distribution (e.g., $pr_F(H$ on toss 1 & H on toss
2$) = pr_F(H$ on toss 1$) pr_F(H$ on toss 2$)$). It is easily verified
that in the epistemic distribution which is a mixture of
these distributions, the tosses are no longer independent.
The intuitive interpretation of this fact is that the outcome
of the first toss gives you some evidence as to which is the
correct "objective" distribution and thus affects the probabilities on the second toss. Thus, in the epistemic distribution, $PR_e(H$ on 2 given H on 1$)$ is greater than $PR_e(H$
on 2 given T on 1$)$. Aside from the intuitive interpretation,
the mathematical moral should be clear: statistical dependence or independence can be created or destroyed by
mixing.

Suppose one has a probability distribution over a series of trials of an experiment (e.g., flips of the coin). The
trials are *independent* if any particular outcome (e.g.,
heads) on one trial is independent of any particular outcome on another trial. The trials are *exchangeable* if the
probability of specified outcomes on n trials does not depend on which trials those n trials are (invariance under
permutation of trials). (Notice that exchangeability is a
typical phenomenon in epistemic probabilities where
none of the trials has yet been performed and where the
names of the trials do not carry any extra information, e.g.,
as to temporal order.) We have seen that a mixture of distributions, each of which makes the trials independent,

may not itself make the trials independent. But a mixture of distributions each of which makes the trials independent will itself make the trials exchangeable.

Suppose we have a finite sequence of trials of an experiment (e.g., flips of a coin). The *relative frequency* of an outcome (e.g., heads) is the fraction of trials that exhibit that outcome. Note that for a finite number of trials the proposition that a certain outcome has a certain relative frequency (compatible with that number of trials) is a proposition in the domain of the probability function, since it is expressible as the disjunction of each conjunction of outcomes of trials which has the desired relative frequency. For example, suppose there are two tosses. Then "Relative frequency of heads is 1/2" is expressed as: (H on 1 and T on 2) or (T on 1 and H on 2). (For an infinite sequence of trials, the *limiting relative frequency*, if it exists, is the limit of the relative frequencies in the initial segments of the sequence of trials. If the probability space is closed under countable conjunction and disjunction, then propositions regarding limiting relative frequencies are also in the probability space.)

We can, then, consider *probabilities conditional on statements of relative frequency*. It is of particular interest to do so in the case of a sequence of exchangeable trials. Let us recall the case in which a coin was flipped twice. Corresponding to "relative frequency of heads equals 1," we have just one case: heads on both tosses. Likewise for "relative frequency of heads equals 0." For "relative frequency of heads equals 1/2," we have two cases: heads on one, tails on two; and tails on one, heads on two. *If the sequence is exchangeable*, these two cases are equally likely. Thus, $PR(H$ on 1 given $RF(H) = 1/2) = PR(H$ on 2 given $RF(H) = 1/2 = 1/2$. The reader can check that this result generalizes. *It is a consequence of exchangeability* that for any outcome, O, and trial, t:

$$PR[O \text{ on } t \text{ given } RF(O) = a] = a$$

This means that we can view any exchangeable distribution as a mixture of relative-frequency distributions. Let the "objective relative-frequency probability" of p when the relative frequency of heads is a, $pr_{RF(H)=a}(p)$, be $PR[p$ given $RF(H) = a]$. So epistemic probability can be thought of as the expectation of "objective relative-frequency probability" as before, and furthermore for individual outcomes the "objective relative-frequency probability" is equal to the relative frequency (e.g., $pr_{RF(H)} = \frac{1}{2}(H$ on 1) $= 1/2$), so that in these cases epistemic probability is the expectation of relative frequency. Notice, however, that this way of representing an exchangeable distribution as a mixture is quite different from the mixtures discussed in the biased coin examples, in that in the "objective" distributions which are elements of the mixture *the trials are no longer independent.* Thus in the case of two tosses of the coin, in the "objective relative-frequency probability" distribution corresponding to relative frequency of heads being 1/2, the probability of tails on two given heads on one is 1; the probability of heads on two given heads on one is 0. (Remember that there *is* no relative frequency of "heads on one, tails on 2," only a relative frequency of heads and one of tails.) *Mathematical moral:* An exchangeable distribution can typically be represented as a mixture in more than one way. *Philosophical moral:* One should be wary of uncritical identification of objective probability with relative frequency. The dependence-of-trials effect in the "objective relative-frequency" distributions is diluted as the number of trials increases and disappears with an infinite number of trials. Thus an infinite exchangeable sequence of trials can be represented as a mixture of "objective relative-frequency" distributions, each of which renders the trials independent (De Finetti's theorem).

Suppose we have a series of trials that are independent and are such that, for any given outcome, the probability of that outcome is the same on each trial (the outcomes are then said to be *identically distributed*). A sequence of flips of a coin known to be fair will again do as an example. We are now interested in the question as to how probable it is that the relative frequency of an outcome (e.g., heads) will fall close (e.g., within .01) to the probability that a trial will exhibit that outcome ($pr(H$ on 1) $= pr(H$ on 2) $= \ldots = 1/2$). The probability that the relative frequency of heads in our example is within .01 of 1/2 can be made arbitrarily close to 1 by taking a large enough number of trials. This result generalizes: *Let* a *be the probability of outcome* O *on a trial. Then for any positive* e_1 *and* e_2, *no matter how small, there is a number of trials,* n, *such that the probability that the relative frequency of* O *is within* e_1 *of* a *in* n *trials, is within* e_2 *of 1.* This is the *weak law of large numbers.* The weak law of large numbers tells us that, if we wait long enough, with high probability the relative frequency of an outcome will approach its probability of being displayed on a trial. A stronger assertion, the *strong law of large numbers,* also holds true of independent and identically distributed sequences of trials. The strong law says not only that the relative frequency of an outcome probably *gets close* to its probability, but also that it probably *gets close and stays close.* That is, for any positive e_1 and e_2, no matter how small, there is a number of trials, n, such that the probability that the relative frequency of O is within e_1 of a in m trials, for every $m \geq n$, is within e_2 of 1.

Appendix 2
Second-Order Probabilities and Fallible Learning[1]

The ascent to second-order probabilities—that is, probabilities of probabilities, permits a much richer theory of learning by conditionalization than that available on the basis of first-order probabilities alone. Let p be a statement of the language on which the first-order distribution is defined. Then, with respect to p, the first-order distribution allows me to represent only learning p for certain (by conditionalization on p) and learning not-p for certain (by conditionalization on not-p). In contrast, the second-order distribution may allow me to conditionalize on $Pr(p) = .0$; or $Pr(p) \geq .9$; or $.8 \geq Pr(p) \geq .9$. In view of the special status of conditionalization, the second-order approach to learning takes on substantial significance.[2]

But the second-order approach will be empty unless some constraints are imposed on how the first- and second-order distributions must cohere. If we allow clashes such as $Pr(p) = 1$, while $Pr[Pr(p) = 0] = 1$, then it is clear that we will not get very far. What is surprising is that very simple and natural constraints get us as far as they do. One almost unavoidable constraint leads straight to the principle that the first-order probabilities must be equal to their second-order expectations.[3] It, together with an additional constraint, leads to the conclusion that con-

1. The results of this appendix were privately circulated in 1975.
2. See P. Teller, "Conditionalization and Observation," *Synthese* (1973):218–58.
3. A principle assumed without justification by some statisticians who do consider second-order distributions. See I. J. Good, *The Estimation of Probabilities* (Cambridge, Mass.: M.I.T. Press, 1965). On the other hand, after seeing this appendix, Richard Jeffrey called my attention to a series of lectures by E. T. Jaynes where he makes essentially the argument from C_2 to the expectation principle. See E. T. Jaynes, *Probability Theory in Science and Engineering*, Colloquium Lectures in Pure and Applied Science, no. 4, Field Research Laboratory, Socony Mobil Oil Co. (Dallas, Texas, 1958), lecture 5, pp. 152–87.

ditionalizing on $Pr(p) = a$ has exactly the same effect on the first-order distribution as would application of Jeffrey's probability kinematics to set $Pr(p) = a$.

THE CONSTRAINTS AND THEIR CONSEQUENCES

Let us start with a language, L_1, which I will assume is closed under negation and countable conjunction and disjunction. I will use lowercase letters (p, q, r) to stand for propositions of L_1. We extend L_1 to L_2 by adding every proposition of the form: $pr(p) \in S$, where S is a Borel set of the real numbers in the interval [0, 1], and p is a proposition of L_1. The constraints I wish to investigate are constraints on the probability distribution on L_2. I shall denote this distribution by the uppercase PR. Use of the uppercase PR then signals that I am talking about the probability distribution on L_2 from outside, whereas the lowercase pr indicates a statement inside L_2 about the probability of a statement in that sublanguage of L_2 that is L_1. (The interpretation of PR and pr will be discussed later.) Let us also assume that PR respects the logical relations of the pr statements: e.g., $pr(p) = .9$ is inconsistent with $pr(p) = .8$, so $PR[pr(p) = .9 \ \& \ pr(p) = .8] = 0$, etc.

The first constraint I want to consider is that if the probability that $pr(p)$ falls in a certain interval[4] is 1, then $PR(p)$ falls in that interval.

Constraint 1 (C_1):
$$PR[pr(p) \in I = 1] \rightarrow PR(p) \in I$$
Requiring that the foregoing coherence property be preserved under conditionalization on a second-order statement gets us:

Constraint 2 (C_2):
$$PR[p \text{ given that } pr(p) \in I] \in I$$
Let us consider first the special case where $PR[pr(p) = x]$ is concentrated at a finite number of values, $a_1, \ldots a_n$ (i.e., where Pr not-$[pr(p) = a_1$ or $\ldots$ or $pr(p) = a_n] = 0$).

---

4. Open, closed, or half-open. This principle cannot, however, be consistently extended to all sets, or even all Borel sets; for consider all sets consisting of the interval with one point removed in the case in which PR is given by a continuous probability distribution function.

Then:

$$PR(p) = \Sigma PR[p \& pr(p) = a_j]$$
$$= \Sigma PR[pr(p) = a_i] \, PR[p \text{ given } pr(p) = a_i]$$
$$= \Sigma \, a_i PR[pr(p) = a_i] \text{ (by } C_2)$$

which is the desired result.

This simple argument generalizes easily to the case in which we have a continuous second-order probability density function, PR^*, such that $PR[pr(p)\epsilon\ (a,b)] = \int_a^b x \, PR^*\ (x)\ dx$.

For any interval, I_i, let $\overline{a_i}$ be $sup\ I_i$ and $\underline{a_i}$ be $inf\ I_i$. For any subdivision, $b_1, \ldots . b_n$, of $[0, 1]$ into intervals, $[0, b_1)$, $[b_1, b_2), \ldots . [b_n, 1]$,[5] let $\overline{PR(p)}$ be $\Sigma PR[pr(p) \epsilon I_i] . \overline{a_i}$ and let $\underline{PR(p)}$ be $\Sigma_i PR[pr(p) \epsilon I_i] \, \underline{a_i}$. Then, for each subdivision, we have $\overline{PR(p)} \geqslant \underline{PR(p)}$ by virtue of C_2. But considering all subdivisions, m, $sup_m \underline{PR(p)} = inf_m \overline{PR(p)} = \int_0^1 x \, PR^*\ (x)$ dx. So $PR(p) = \int_0^i x \, PR^*\ (x)\ dx.$[6]

If constraint C_2 is satisfied, then PR(p) *is equal to the* PR-*expected value of* pr(p).

To go further, we need to introduce another constraint: *Constraint 3 (C_3):*

$$Pr[q \text{ given } p \& pr(p) = a] =$$
$$Pr[q \text{ given } p]\text{[7]}$$

It is not so plausible for C_3 as for C_2 that it be a universal constraint, but it is certainly plausible that C_3 hold in a large number of cases (e.g., the probability of a Geiger counter click given that the probability of radioactive decay is *a, and that the atom did decay,* is equal to the probability of a click given that it did decay). Now suppose that we wish to represent learning p with less than certainty by conditionalizing on $pr(p) = a$ for some value of *a* less than 1. The effect of the acquisition of such uncertain information on *a* shows up in $Pr[q$ given $pr(p) = a]$.

---

5. Since the distribution function is continuous, taking $[b_n, 1]$ instead of $[b_n, 1)$ will make no difference.

6. Generalization to the mixed case where $PR\ pr(p) = x$ is partly concentrated and partly given by a continuous probability density function is easy, but note that the nature of C_2 does not permit full generalization to the Lebesgue integral.

7. There are more general versions, such as $PR[q$ given $p \& pr(p) \epsilon I]$ $= PR[q$ given $p]$, that might be considered, but I will make the point with the principle as stated.

This equals:

$$PR[q \& p \& pr(p) = a] + Pr[q \& \sim p \& pr(p) =$$
$$a]/Pr[pr(p) = a] = PR[pr(p) = a] \, PR[p \text{ given } pr(p)$$
$$= a] \, PR[q \text{ given } p \& pr(p) = a]/PR[pr(p) = a] +$$
$$PR[pr(p) = a] \, PR[\sim p \text{ given } pr(p) = a] \, PR[q \text{ given}$$
$$\sim p \& pr(p) = a]/PR[pr(p) = a]$$

By C_2 this reduces to:

$$a \, PR[q \text{ given } p \& pr(p) = a] + (1 - a) \, PR[q \text{ given}$$
$$\sim p \& pr(p) = a]$$

And by C_3 this reduces to:

$$a \, PR[q \text{ given } p] + (1 - a) \, PR[q \text{ given } \sim p]$$

This means that under these constraints, conditionalizing on $pr(p) = a$ has the same effect on an arbitrary first-order proposition, q, as quasi-conditionalizing á la Jeffrey on p at level a. That is, under these constraints, the second-order account of learning with less than certainty, and Jeffrey's first-order account, are in agreement.

INTERPRETATION OF THE PROBABILITIES AND THE CONSTRAINTS

The plausibility of the constraints will, of course, depend on the nature of the first- and second-order probabilities involved. One natural interpretation would be to regard *PR* as specifying *rational degree of belief* and *pr* as referring to *propensities*.[8] Then C_2 would be a plausible inductive rule for assimilating propensity information. However, C_3, on this interpretation, is not universally valid, since the existence of a certain propensity value with regard to p might be evidence for or against q. (E.g., we have two coins. Coin 1, a copper coin, is fair. Coin 2, a silver coin, is biased 2-to-1 in favor of heads. One of the two coins is selected at random and tossed. The rational degree of belief that the coin tossed was made of copper given that it came up heads is not equal to the rational degree of belief that it was made of copper given that it came

8. This sort of approach is taken by David Lewis in "A Subjectivist's Guide to Objective Chance," in R. Jeffrey, ed., *Studies in Inductive Logic and Probability*, vol. 2 (Berkeley and Los Angeles: University of California Press, 1979). C_2 + resiliency = Lewis's "Principal Principle."

up heads and had a propensity of 2/3 to come up heads. To take a somewhat more interesting example: the quantum-mechanical probabilities of a measurement result may carry information about the state of the system *before* the measurement, over and above the information given by the measurement itself. On the other hand, assuming that the measurement really does collapse the wave packet, *subsequent* states will depend only on the outcome of the measurement, and thus C_3 will be satisfied. Likewise, C_3 will be satisfied for q subsequent to p in any Markov chain.)

On the other hand, both PR and pr might be given a degree-of-belief reading. This could be done in two ways. One would be to take PR as a rational degree of belief and pr as some sort of *objectified* degree of belief. This, of course, *is* the propensity reading, if propensities are interpreted as objectified degrees of belief, as I have suggested in chapter IA. Here C_2 seems unexceptionable, but C_3 is implausible in the same cases as before.

The other way would be to identify PR and pr as degrees of belief of an agent who does not know his own mind (at least does not know exactly what degrees of belief he attaches to propositions).[9] This idea may seem bizarre, or even contradictory, to those accustomed to epistemology in the Cartesian mode, but such discomforts should subside if we think of belief as dispositional. For this interpretation, PR and pr refer to the same thing: degrees of belief of a subject who has degrees of belief about his degrees of belief. It is one thing not to know one's own mind for certain, and another thing to be deluded about it. The agent who violates C_1 is certain that his degree of belief in p is in I, although it isn't. C_1 is thus, on this interpretation, a minimal self-knowledge condition. The agent who has minimal self-knowledge in the sense of C_1 and is set up to maintain it after conditionalization on sentence of the form $PR(p) \epsilon I$ will satisfy C_2. C_3 describes an

9. See Richard Jeffrey's discussion in "Preference among Preferences," *Journal of Philosophy* vol. 71, no. 13 (July, 1974):377–91. See also D. Jamison's discussion of second-order personal probabilities in "Bayesian Information Usage," in J. Hintikka and P. Suppes, eds., *Information and Inference* (Dordrecht: Reidel, 1970).

agent who is set up so that if he learns and conditionalizes on both the fact that his own degree of belief in p is a and the fact that p is true,[10] he will give a first-order proposition, q, the same final degree of belief that he would if he conditionalized only on the fact of the matter, p, and ignored his degree of belief in p. In general, this sounds like a kind of intellectual virtue; but, again, the agent's degree of belief in p is part of the world and may, in special cases, be correlated with q.

Urn Models

What is the probability of drawing a red ball, conditional on the hypothesis that it was drawn at random from an urn containing 50 red balls and 50 black balls? (A *random* draw is one in which every member of the population has an equal chance of being drawn.) It is clear that here we are being asked for the value of a probability conditional on a probabilistic statement. If we denote the probability involved in the notion of a random sample as pr and the probability being queried as PR, then the correct solution will invoke C_2. We will need to know that PR(red drawn given pr red drawn $= 1/2) = 1/2$. Higher-order probabilities are involved if one selects the urn from which the ball is drawn by random sampling from a population of urns, and so forth. From this point of view, second-order probabilities and principle C_2 are ubiquitous. Of course, one can get the same effect by introducing *drawn-from-the-urn-by-random-sampling* into the first-order language, together with the appropriate probabilities conditional on it that one would get by principle C_2 on the earlier approach.

That is, we can represent the second-order probabilities within a first-order approach by expanding the first-order language. For every possible pr-distribution, pr_i, we introduce a new first-order statement, w_i, and let

10. One might suspect that someone who conditionalizes on p & $PR(p) = a$ where $1 > a > 0$ would land himself in a probability distribution which would embarrass him with respect to 1 and 2, with $PR[p$ given $PR(p) = a] = 1$ rather than a. But the conditionalization takes us from an initial distribution, Pr_i, to a final one, Pr_f, and it is no embarrassment that $PR_f[p$ given $PR_i(p) = a] = 1$.

$Pr(p$ given $w_i) = pr_i(p).$[11] (If we are lucky we may find such a w_i already within our first-order language.) Within the first-order model, the principle that a first-order probability is equal to its second-order expectation reduces to the theorem on total probability. Such first-order models are good medicine for acrophobia.

Suppose we have 100 urns, with urn n containing n red balls and 100-n white balls. An urn is selected at random and a ball selected at random from it. But, furthermore, the balls put into the urns were drawn at random from master urns of red and white balls. The master urn of red balls contained 1 million ivory balls and 2 million plastic ones. The master urn of white balls contained 2 million ivory and 1 million plastic. Then, letting "$p =$ white balls drawn" and "$q =$ plastic balls drawn" be the first-order propositions, and interpreting the urn talk in a higher-order way, we find that both C_2 and C_3 are satisfied.[12]

---

11. The w_is form a partition.

12. For further development of the ideas suggested in this appendix, see my "Higher-Order Degrees of Belief," forthcoming in H. Mellor, ed., *Prospects for Pragmatism: Essays on F. P. Ramsey* (Cambridge: Cambridge University Press, 1980).

Appendix 3
Iterated Probability Conditionals and Lewis's Triviality Proof

INTRODUCTION

By the *inferential probability conditional*, $p \rightarrow q$, I mean a conditional which has as its probability value, the probability value the q would have after conditionalizing on p. Thus, for conditional-free p, q, it follows that the value of the conditional is the associated conditional probability:

I. $V(p \rightarrow q) = Pr(p \& q)/Pr(p)$

But since we know $V(p \rightarrow q)$ in any given probability distribution over conditional-free sentences, we know its value in a distribution gotten by conditionalizing on (conditional-free) r. That is, we know $V[r \rightarrow (p \rightarrow q)]$, which turns out to be:

II. $V[r \rightarrow (p \rightarrow q)] = V[r \rightarrow (p \& q)]/V(r \rightarrow p) = V[(r \& p) \rightarrow q]$[1]

It is customary to call a conditional which obeys I a *probability conditional*. Some investigators stopped short of assuming II. But it is clear that the conception of the *inferential* probability conditional forces II as well as I.

Although the inferential probability conditional permits iterations in the consequent, as in II, it leaves us without any clear conception of iteration in the antecedent, such as $(p \rightarrow q) \rightarrow r$, because we have no clear conception of what it might be to conditionalize on a conditional.

One might be tempted to push through this impasse by applying the laws of the probability calculus to sentences *containing* conditionals as well as conditional-free sentences. Then Bayes' theorem immediately gives us $V[(p \rightarrow q) \rightarrow r]$ in terms of things we already know, i.e., $V(r)V[r \rightarrow (p \rightarrow q)]/V(p \rightarrow q)$.

More precisely, what is assumed is that we can enrich sentential logic with inferential probability conditionals,

---

1. Providing $Pr(r \& p) \neq 0$.

such that it is closed under conditional formation, and the normal truth-functional operations, and such that:

    a. it retains a Boolean structure;

    b. the values of the enlarged set of sentences behave as probabilities on that structure;

    c. the ratio measure of (I), $V(p \to q) = V(p \& q)/V(p)$, continues to hold good when p and q themselves contain conditionals.

Lewis's triviality proof shows that this assumption is, in all but some trivial probability distributions, false.

LEWIS'S TRIVIALITY PROOF[2]

Lewis invites us to do a Boolean expansion on our conditional in terms of its consequent.

$$(1)\quad V(p \to q) = V\left\{[(q \& (p \to q)]\right.$$
$$\left. \mathbf{v}\,[\sim q \& (p \to q)]\right\} \text{ Boolean exp.}$$

$$(2)\qquad\qquad = V[q \& (p \to q)]$$
$$+ V[\sim q \& (p \to q)] \text{ additivity}$$

$$(3)\qquad\qquad = V(q)\,V[q \to (p \to q)]$$
$$+ V(\sim q)\,V[\sim q \to (p \to q)] \qquad C$$

$$(4)\qquad\qquad = V(q)\,V[(p \& q) \to q]$$
$$+ V(\sim q)\,V[(p \& \sim q) \to q] \qquad \text{II}$$

$$(5)\qquad\qquad = V(q)\,1 + V(\sim q)\,O \qquad\qquad\qquad I$$

$$(6)\, Pr(p \& q)/Pr(p) = Pr(q)$$

Thus we are forced to restrictions on *conditional free* sentences which can be satisfied only in trivial cases.

AN ALGEBRAIC FACT OF LIFE

A simple algebraic fact stands behind both the Lewis's triviality proof and the need to consider a fundamental partition in the analysis of probabilistic causality. The fact is that mixtures (weighted averages) of quotients are not in general equal to the corresponding quotients of mix-

2. My version. Compare Lewis, "Probabilities of Conditionals and Conditional Probabilities," *Philosophical Review*, vol. 85, no. 3 (1976):297–315.

tures. This has the consequence for probability theory that mixing and conditionalization do not commute.

To see what I mean, recall that mixtures of sums are sums of mixtures in the following sense:

$$[\alpha(a + b)] + [(1 - \alpha)(c + d)] = [\alpha a + (1 - \alpha)c] + [\alpha b + (1 - \alpha)d]$$

But it is not in general true that mixtures of quotients are quotients of mixtures. That is, the following does not hold generally:

A Mistaken Principle:

$$[\alpha(a/b) + (1 - \alpha)(c/d)] = \{[\alpha a + (1 - \alpha)c]/[\alpha b + (1 - \alpha)d]\}$$

Counterexample 1:

$$\alpha = 2/3; a = .1; b = .2; c = .3; d = .4$$

Counterexample 2:

$$a = 0; b = 1, c = .1; d = .1; \alpha = ?$$

To see that this fact is at the heart of the triviality result, consider that the assumptions of the triviality proof give us:

$$Pr(p \to q) = Pr(z)Pr[z \to (p \to q)]$$
$$+ Pr(\sim z)Pr[\sim z \to (p \to q)]$$
$$= Pr(z) Pr_z(p \to q) + Pr(\sim z) Pr_{\sim z}(p \to q)$$

(where Pr_z is the probability distribution gotten from Pr by conditionalization on z)

$$= Pr(z)[Pr_z(p \& q)/Pr_z(p)]$$
$$+ [1 - Pr(z)][Pr_{\sim z}(p \& q)/Pr_{\sim z}(p)]$$

which is a mixture of ratios. But we also know, from the probability calculus:

$$Pr(q \text{ given } p) = Pr(p \& q)/Pr(p)$$
$$= \frac{\{Pr(z)Pr_z(p \& q) + [1 - Pr(z)]Pr_{\sim z}(p \& q)\}}{\{Pr(z)Pr_z(p) + [1 - Pr(z)]Pr_{\sim z}(p)\}}$$

which is the corresponding ratio of mixtures. The two ways of determining $Pr(p \to q)$ are not, in general, equal.

The same fact is behind the importance of including all the causally relevant factors in the partition when evaluating probabilistic causation. Let $C_1, \ldots C_{n+1}$ be the factors causally relevant to $Pr(G \text{ given } F)$. Suppose we leave out a factor, and only partition according to $C_1, \ldots C_n$. Looking at probabilities within cells in this partition is equivalent to looking at mixtures relative to the missing factor. That is, letting P be some element of the partition generated by $C_1, \ldots . C_n$:

$$Pr_P(G \text{ given } F) = Pr_P(G \& F)/Pr_P(F)$$

$$= \frac{Pr_P(C_{n+1})Pr_{P \& c_{n+1}}(G \& F) + Pr_P(\sim C_{n+1})Pr_{P \& \sim c_{n+1}}(G \& F)}{Pr_P(C_{n+1})Pr_{P \& c_{n+1}}(F) + Pr_P(\sim C_{n+1})Pr_{P \& \sim c_{n+1}}(F)}$$

If we could be assured that this ratio of mixtures was a mixture of the ratios that represented the conditional probabilities within the two cells obtained by subdividing P by the missing causal factor C_{n+1}, that is, if the foregoing were equal to:

$$Pr_P(C_{n+1}) Pr_{P \& c_{n+1}} (G \text{ given } F)$$
$$+ Pr(\sim C_{n+1}) Pr_{P \& \sim c_{n+1}} (G \text{ given } F)$$

then the partition that left out a causal factor would still give us useful causal information. But this is just what we do not have, in general. In fact, the smoking example of chapter IIC shows that $PR_P(G \text{ given } F)$ need not even lie between $Pr_{P \& c_{n+1}} (G \text{ given } F)$ and $Pr_{P \& \sim c_{n+1}} (G \text{ given } F)$.

CONDITIONALIZING ON CONDITIONAL PROBABILITIES

We might take as the moral of the story that there is simply no sense in conditionalizing on the probability conditional—or, equivalently, in conditionalizing on a conditional probability—nor is there any clear sense to applying the truth-functional connectives to probability conditionals, since the values of probability conditionals are not probabilities of truth but rather ratios of probabilities of truth. But is this too hasty? Within the framework of second-order probabilities developed in appendix 2, we have a device available which corresponds roughly to the vague idea of conditionalizing on a conditional probability. We can conditionalize on the statement that a conditional probability is 1 or near 1. Thus, we could take the value of $(p \rightarrow q) \rightarrow r$ to be:

$$PR[r \text{ given } pr(q \text{ given } p) = 1]$$

or

$$PR[r \text{ given } pr(q \text{ given } p) \geq 1 - \epsilon] \text{ for appropriate } \epsilon$$

or the limit as ϵ approaches 0 of the foregoing (providing it exists). A suitable hierarchy of higher-order probabilities would thus permit a kind of extension of the inferential probability conditional to iterations in the antecedent. There is a slight artificiality in the approach, however, since $PR[pr(q \text{ given } p) = 1]$ need not equal $PR(q \text{ given } p)$.[3] It is just this that saves us from the triviality proof since:

$$V(p \to q) = V\{[(p \to q) \& p] \lor [(p \to q) \& \sim p]\}$$

is meaningless and

$$V(p \to q) = PR[pr(q \text{ given } p = 1 \& p)$$
$$\lor pr(q \text{ given } p = 1 \& \sim p)]$$

is, in general, false. The artificiality does not deprive the approach of all interest, however, since the most natural sense of learning the probability conditional *interpreted as inference ticket* is learning that the associated conditional probability is high.

The second-order approach just sketched is a special case of the following schema:

Values:

If p is conditional-free, its value in a given probability distribution (over the conditional-free sentences) $[Pr_i]$ is just its probability, $Pr_i(p)$.

The value of a conditional, $p \to q$, in $[Pr_i]$ is the value that q has in the distribution obtained from $[Pr_i]$ by conditionalizing on p, $C_p[Pr_i]$.

Generalized Conditionalization:

The distribution obtained from $[Pr_i]$ by generalized conditionalization, $C_p[Pr_i]$, is that probability distribution which conservatively maximizes the value of p.

As put, the schema looks rather Stalnakerish, and it is, with possible probability distributions playing the role of possible worlds. One might even put Stalnakerish constraints on the notion of conservative maximization:

(1) If $Pr_i(p) = 1$, then $C_p[Pr_i] = [Pr_i]$ (conservative bias)

(2) If $C_p[Pr_i] = [Pr_j]$ then $Pr_j(p) = 1$ (maximization)

(3) If $C_p[Pr_i] = [Pr_j]$ and $Pr_j(q) = 1$ and   (consistency)
      $C_q[Pr_i] = [Pr_k]$ and $Pr_k(p) = 1$ then
      $C_p[Pr_i] = C_q[Pr_i]$

Satisfaction of these constraints gives what Lewis calls an *eligible probability-revision conditional.* And Lewis

---

3. Likewise for the alternative suggestions.

shows that the Stalnaker conditional can be regarded as generated by such probability-revision conditionals, where such conditionals are restricted to *opinionated* (0–1) probability distributions, which are the characteristic distributions of possible worlds (conceived of as sets of propositions).

For an eligible probability-revision conditional to be *inferential* probability conditional in the sense of I, it must satisfy an additional constraint. Generalized conditionalization must indeed be a generalization of conditionalization; *if p is conditional-free,* conservative maximization must be interpreted as conditionalization on p in the sense of the Kolmogoroff ratio measure:

Inferential Probability Conditional (IPC):

If $C_p[Pr_i] = [Pr_j]$ then for any $q\, Pr_j(q) = Pr_i(p\,\&\,q)/$ $Pr_i(p)$ (for conditional-free p)

Notice that IPC is compatible with the three Stalnakerish constraints given above. Notice also that IPC puts no further constraints over and above these three on opinionated distributions. For if $Pr(p) = 0$, the ratio in question is undefined and IPC does not apply, while if $Pr(p) = 1$, IPC is a consequence of constraint 1 (conservative bias).

The inferential probability conditional *is* compatible with the Stalnaker conditional. Stalnaker's attempted marriage between the two failed because of the wrong strategy. He attempted to identify the value of the probability conditional with the probability of truth of the Stalnaker conditional. The match fell afoul of the Lewis triviality proof. Lewis has success with a different arrangement. The truth value of the Stalnaker conditional is identified with the probability value of an eligible probability-revision conditional in an opinionated probability distribution which corresponds to the world in question. Restricting the eligible probability conditionals to inferential probability conditionals does not induce any real restriction in the compatible Stalnaker conditionals, since for any eligible probability conditional we can generate an inferential probability conditional that is equivalent on opinionated distributions, essentially by filling in the undefined cases of conditional probability to give the right results. If, on the other hand, we had some well-defined notion of $Pr(p \& q)/Pr(p)$, where $Pr(p) = 0$, some well-defined notion of conditionalizing on a condition of zero probability, perhaps by taking limits or by utilizing nonstandard analysis, as in appendix 4, then we could take IPC in such a way that it would put real restrictions on the compatible Stalnaker conditionals.

Iterated Conditionals in English

The probability conditional and the Stalnaker conditional are both grounded in the idea of an inferential conditional, but they apply that root idea in different ways. The inferential probability conditional evaluates $p \to q$ by looking at the value that q would have after revising our degrees of belief so as to conservatively set $Pr(p) = 1$, starting from our current probability distribution. The Stalnaker conditional evaluates $p \to q$ (as to truth) in the same way, but starting from a different distribution, an opinionated distribution that matches the world. The Stalnaker conditional can be thought of as an inferential probability conditional that is totally objectified.

Which conditional makes the best sense for our use of iterated conditionals in English? My feeling is that we use both. The most obvious logical difference for iterations is that in almost all cases the inferential probability obeys Ellis's principle:

$r \to (p \to q)$ is equivalent to $(r \& p) \to q$

by virtue of II, while the Stalnaker conditional evaluates the two quite differently. How is this possible, given that the Stalnaker conditional *is* the inferential probability conditional applied to opinionated probability distributions? The catch is that the proof of II requires that $Pr(r \& p)$ be non-zero, a small requirement for most cases of the inferential probability conditional, but a big one when applied to opinionated distributions. Indeed, if r and p are both true, the Stalnaker conditional will assign the same truth value to $r \to (p \to q)$ and to $(r \& p) \to q$, but these are hardly the cases of prime interest.

Examples of such iterated probability conditionals are fairly rare in English, but, among the examples that come to mind, Ellis's principle seems fairly strong. Consider:

Indicative:

> If this sample *is* burning green, then if it *is* a sodium salt
>
> (a) it *is* a sodium salt burning green
>
> (b) it *is* burning yellow

Subjunctive:

> If this sample *were* burning green, then if it *were* a sodium salt
>
> (a) it *would* be a sodium salt burning green
>
> (b) it *would* be burning yellow

I think that the natural interpretation in each case could choose the first continuation as trivially true and reject the second as trivially false. Nevertheless, in the subjunctive case (though not in the indicative) I can imagine appropriate promptings and side remarks that would lead me to take some variant of the counterfactual in the Stalnaker way:

> If this sample were burning green (say it was barium) then it would still be true that had it been sodium it would have burned yellow.

The question of what cues in English lead you to take a counterfactual one way rather than the other is, I think, a very complicated business.

Appendix 4
Nonstandard Analysis and Infinitesimal Probabilities

From Henkin's completeness proof we know that first-order logic is *compact*. If a set of sentences is such that every finite subset of it has a model, then the set in question has a model. The Henkin proof in no way depends on the assumption that the set of sentences or the set of constants of the language in question is denumerable. (That every set with the property that every finite subset of it has a model can be extended to a maximal set with that property, holds for sets of arbitrary cardinality by transfinite induction. The union of a chain of sets with that property must have that property.) It does depend on the sentences of the language being of finite length, and the logical constants being limited to the truth functions, identity, and first-order quantifiers. (For the proof that the model associated with the maximal consistent set is a model of each sentence in it is by induction on the length of the sentences.) Thus by Henkin's proof (or by a variation on it on the level of the models, the ultraproduct construction) we see that we have compactness for rich, nondenumerable first-order languages (e.g., for a first-order language with a name for every real number and operation, and relation symbols for every operation and relation on the reals). Compactness fails for higher-order quantification if second-order quantifiers are given the "natural" interpretation of having as their domain the power set of the domain of the first-order quantifiers, and so forth. Given the natural interpretation of second-order quantifiers, we can in second-order logic write a sentence, A, which has all the truths of arithmetic as logical consequences. Then $\{A, (\exists x) (\sim Fx), F1, F2, F3, \ldots\}$ is an infinite set which has no model but such that each finite subset of it has a model. But if we relax the interpretation of higher-order quantifiers, so that a permissible model (Henkin calls these *general* models) results whenever the higher-order quantifiers are taken as ranging over a *subset* of their natural domain, then the Henkin strategy for constructing the domain of a model from the constants occurring in a maximally consistent set of sentences succeeds for higher-order domains as well. In this sense, higher-order logic with the usual quantifier rules is complete and compact. But, once general models are admitted, higher-order logic cannot categorically characterize arithmetic anymore than first-order logic can. Nonstandard general models of arithmetic (and analysis) are now possible. It is a mark of Abraham Robinson's genius that he turned this logical defect into a powerful tool of discovery.

NONSTANDARD ARITHMETIC

For the time being we will restrict our attention to first-order logic. Let us choose as our language of arithmetic a first-order language containing a name for every number operation; symbols for successor, plus, and times; and a relational symbol for less than. Let *Arithmetic* be the set of all true sentences of this language. Take a variable, y. Consider the theory Arithmetic $\cup \{ y \neq 0, y \neq 1, y \neq 2, \ldots \}$. By compactness, this theory has a model (and by the Lowenheim-Skolem theorem a denumerable model). Designate the elements of this model *numbers** and in general designate the denotation assigned by this model to any constant by the constant followed by an asterisk. Thus *less than** is the extension assigned by the nonstandard model to the less-than relation.

Since the axioms for a linear ordering are first-order, and since the nonstandard model *is* a model of arithmetic, *less than** linear orders the *numbers**. Since the claim that zero is the least number is a first-order truth, and since the nonstandard model *is* a model, 0^* is the *least** *number**. Likewise, 1^* is the *next-to-least** *number**, and so forth. The nonstandard model, considered under the order relation *less than**, begins with an ω-series: $1^*, 2^*, 3^*. \ldots$. The elements of this series together with the asterisked operations and relations on them are isomorphic to the numbers, because the nonstandard model is a model (e.g., since "$2 + 2 = 4$" is a sentence of Arithmetic, $2^* + {}^*2^* = 4^*$.) We may then, for all intents and purposes, call the elements assigned as denotations to the numerals, $1^*, 2^*, 3^*, \ldots$, the numbers (or, for emphasis, the standard numbers) and the structure consisting of them together with the restriction to them of the asterisked relations and operations, the standard model of arithmetic. The nonstandard model is, then, an end-extension of the standard model.

The inclusion of one nonstandard element in the model forces the inclusion of many others, since Arithmetic requires that every number have a successor greater than itself. Let us partition the numbers* into equivalence classes by considering the equivalence relation differs* by a standard number (i.e., there is a standard, z, such that x $+^* z = y$ or $y +^* z = x$). Call these equivalence classes Blocks. The standard numbers form one Block. There must be at least one greater* Block since there are nonstandard numbers. But for every nonstandard Block there must be a greater Block to which we may pass by multiplying* by 2^*. For if 2^* times* y were in the same Block as y, then by the definition of same Block they would differ* by a standard number, but they differ* by y ("Twice y less y is y" is a sentence of Arithmetic), contradicting the assumption that y is nonstandard. A like argument will show that there is no least Block and that the Blocks are densely ordered by less than*. Consider the operation, halb, of approximate division by two. Halb d = c iff $2d = c$ or $2d + 1 = c$. Now if d is in a nonstandard Block, halb* d is in a lesser* nonstandard Block. For if they were in the same Block, d would have to be standard, contrary to hypothesis. And if halb* d were standard, d would be also, contrary to hypothesis. Likewise, between* any two Blocks there must be another, for if c and d are in different Blocks halb* $c +^* d$ must be in another Block (all of whose members are) between* c and d. The Blocks must then be ordered with dense order: no first, no last element. Inside the Blocks, we may rely on the sentences of Arithmetic that say that every number has a successor and that nothing comes after the number but before its successor, and that every number other than zero has a predecessor, and that no number comes after its predecessor but before it. This, together with the constraints of the equivalence relation defining the *Blocks*, tells us that internally each *Block* is ordered as the negative integers, zero, and positive integers. If we confine ourselves to *countable* nonstandard models, this then fixes the order type of the nonstandard model.

NONSTANDARD RATIONALS

Let the language for the rationals contain a name for each rational; operations of addition, multiplication, and division; a less-than relation; and the predicate "is a natural number." Let RAT consist of all the true sentences of this language. Consider the theory $RAT \cup (y > r_1, y > r_2, y > r_i,$ . . .) for some enumeration (I) of the rationals. Every finite subset of this set has a model in the rationals, so by compactness it does as well. (And, again, by the Lowenheim-Skolem theorem, it has a countable model.) Once more we will identify the denotata of the r_is as the standard rationals. So the nonstandard model contains an infinite element *greater than* * all the standard rationals. Multiply it by its divisor to get an infinite natural *number* * and the argument establishing the structure of the nonstandard natural *numbers* * can proceed as with nonstandard arithmetic. The countable nonstandard model of the rationals is an extension of the countable nonstandard model of arithmetic. Since a proposition of RAT asserts that every rational has a reciprocal and that taking the reciprocals of two numbers inverts the order, the infinite elements must have reciprocals which are *less than* * any positive standard rational and *greater than* * 0 *. That is, we have infinitesimal elements. Notice that we have quite a rich structure of infinitesimals due to the interaction of closure under addition, multiplication, and division. Thus, if we have an infinite element, N, we have the corresponding infinitesimal $\epsilon = 1$ * $/N$, as well as ϵ^{2} *, ϵ^{3} *, 1 * $/N$ $+$ * ϵ, etc. Let us say that a nonstandard rational is *finite* if it is bounded above and below by standard rationals other than zero *, *infinite* if it is *greater than* * any finite number, and *infinitesimal* if it is *less than** any finite number. Let us say that two nonstandard rationals are of the same *Order* if their quotient is finite. *Orders* provide a coarser partitioning of the infinite elements than the *Blocks* considered in the discussion of nonstandard arithmetic. In fact, . . . $N/4, N/2, N, 2N, 4N$ . . . are all of the same *Order*. Nevertheless, for every infinite *Order*, there is a *greater** one. N^{2*} is greater than N and of a different *Order*.[1] Furthermore, for every infinite *Order* there is a *lesser** one. Let us say that y is an *approximate square root of* x if $x \leqslant^* v^{2*} \leqslant^* x +^* 1^*$. A sentence of *RAT* says that everything has at least one approximate square root.[2] An approximate square root of an infinite number cannot be finite, since the finite numbers are closed under addition and multiplication, and it cannot be of the same *Order* as x since its square is. Along the same lines, we can show that *between** each two infinite *Orders* there is another one using as the leading idea "an approximate geometric mean." Since two infinite elements are of the same *Order* just in case their reciprocals are, and since the *Order* of the reciprocals is the inverse of the *Order* of the infinite elements, this shows that the *Orders* of infinitesimals (excluding zero) are densely ordered with no first or last element.

Nonstandard Analysis

In the preceding sections we took pains to keep to a denumerable model, but here we will not, so we may allow the luxury of starting with a truly opulent first-order language. Let our language of analysis include a name, c_r, for every real, r; a relational symbol for every relation on the reals; and an operational symbol for every operation on the reals. Let *ANA* be the set of all true sentences of this language, and consider the theory which is the union of *ANA* with the set of all sentences of the form $c_r < y$ for

1. Notice that this shows that we did not look at *all* the nonstandard natural numbers in the argument which established the order type of the denumerable nonstandard model of arithmetic.
2. Note that we could approximate *infinitely* close to $\sqrt{2}$, for instance, since a translation of $(z)(x)(x \neq \supset (\exists y)(|y^2 - x| \leqslant z))$ is in RAT.

each real r. By compactness, this theory has a model, a nonstandard model of the reals. Again, the function which maps each real, r, on to c_r*, the denotation in the nonstandard model of its name, is an isomorphism. Each nonstandard model contains an isomorphic copy of the reals. Working within the model we will simply call these the *standard reals*. The denotation of the less-than relation, <*, totally orders the nonstandard reals, R*, since the axioms of total order are first-order. The nonstandard reals form a field (that is, $\langle R^*, 0^*, 1^*, +^*, \cdot^* \rangle$ is a field), since the properties of a field are expressible by first-order axioms. It need not have properties which require second-order axioms for their expression. It is not Archimedean. It does not have the least-upper-bound property. The standard reals provide an example of a set in the model which has an upper bound but no least upper bound.

If the set of standard reals which satisfies F is unbounded in the standard reals, then *F has an infinite element in the nonstandard model. For then the first-order sentence $(x)[Fx \supset (\exists y) (Fy \text{ and } y > x)]$ is in ANA, and taking x as the infinite element that we constructed with the model forces F to contain an infinite element. Thus the set of nonstandard natural numbers, N*, and the set of nonstandard rationals, Ra*, contain infinite elements. The statement that every real is bounded by natural numbers is in ANA. So we can repeat the arguments of the previous sections to show that *Blocks* and *Orders* of infinite elements are densely ordered with no first or last elements, and likewise for the infinitesimals (excluding 0*). This, however, no longer settles the question of order type since the model is nondenumerable.

Let us say that x if *infinitely close to* y if $|x - {}^*y|^*$ is infinitesimal. Infinitely close to (symbolically $\simeq$) is an equivalence relation on R*. For standard reals $r \simeq s$ implies $r = s$, since zero is the only standard infinitesimal. If $x \not\simeq y$ and at least one of them is finite, then there is a standard real, q, between x and y. For suppose that $0^* \leqslant^* x \leqslant^* y$. By the definition of $\simeq$ there is a standard, b, such that $0^* \leqslant^* b \leqslant^* y -^* x$. Choose the least standard integer,

m, such that $mb >^* x$. Then $x <^* mb <^* y$. *Every finite nonstandard real is infinitely close to a unique standard real.* For consider the set of all standard reals less than x. It has a standard upper bound (since x is finite), so it has a least upper bound, r, in the standard reals. Then x is infinitely close to r, since there is no standard q between x and r. Furthermore, r is the unique standard real that is infinitely close to x; since if y is infinitely close to r, then by transitivity y is infinitely close to x, and if y as well as x is standard, then they can be infinitely close only if identical.

Let F be a function on the reals. Then the standard definition of "F converges to a at b" is:

$$(\epsilon)[\epsilon <0 \supset (\exists\delta)(x)(|x - a| \neq 0 \;\&\; |x - a| < \delta \supset |b - F_*| < \epsilon].$$

The nonstandard definition is: F converges to a at b iff whenever x is infinitely close to (but different from) a, $F^*(x)$ is infinitely close to b. The two definitions are equivalent. *The standard definition implies the nonstandard one:* Suppose that the standard definition holds. Then its true instances are in ANA. That is, for a fixed real number, E, greater than zero, we will have a sentence:

$$(x)[|x - a| < D \supset |b - F(x)| < E]$$

in ANA where D is a fixed real number. These sentences must be satisfied in the nonstandard model. Then if x is infinitely close to a, for each such sentence we have $|x -^* a^*|^* <^* D^*$ and thus $|b^* -^* F^*(x)|^* <^* E^*$. But since we have such a sentence for every standard real with E naming that real, $F^*(x)$ is infinitely close to b. *The nonstandard definition implies the standard one.* Suppose the nonstandard definition holds. Then consider any instantiation of the standard definition to a fixed standard real, E:

$$(\exists\delta)(x)[|x - a| < \delta \supset |b - F(x)| < E]$$

This sentence is true in the nonstandard model, as can be seen by choosing δ infinitesimal. It is a first-order sentence, so it holds in the standard model. Thus, reasoning about the behavior of infinitesimals in the nonstandard model can yield truths about limits in the standard model. Many of the arguments of Newton and Leibniz can, from our vantage point, now be seen to have just this character.

Robinson's interest in the nonstandard model was centered on its use as a tool to prove theorems about the standard model.

Nonstandard Measure Theory

Here we assume we have a nonstandard general model of analysis, where the first-order language of analysis of the previous section is extended to type theory. (Types are taken as follows: The set of types is the smallest set such that (1) 0 is a type and (2) if $t_1, t_2, \ldots t_n$ are types, then $(t_1, t_2, \ldots t_n)$ is a type.) The general model allows the higher-order quantifiers to have as their domain some subset of their "natural domain."[3] For instance, quantifiers of type (0) may not range over all subsets of R^*. The elements of the model that are within the domains of the quantifiers are called *internal*.

A relation $R(xy)$ is said to be *finitely satisfiable* if for every set of elements in its domain, $a_1, a_2, \ldots a_n$, there is a y such that $R(a_i, y)$ holds for each a_i. If R is a finitely satisfiable relation on the standard reals (or the higher-order structure built up from them), then, by compactness, a nonstandard model can be found such that it contains an element, y, such that given any standard x in the domain of R, $R^*(x^*, y)$. The arguments of the previous sections that established the existence of nonstandard models with infinite elements are a special case, with the finitely satisfiable relation taken us $<$. The nonstandard model can be arranged to contain elements such as y which simultaneously satisfy the relation R for all standard elements in their domain, for as many finitely satisfiable relations as you please, since the set of sentences $\{R_j(a_{ij}, y_j)$ for every a_{ij} in the standard domain of $R_j\}$ still has the property that every finite subset of it has a standard model.

The leading idea of nonstandard measure theory is the use of *finite samples. The second-order predicate "is finite" has as its extension in the nonstandard model a set

3. The "natural domain" of the quantifiers of higher type induced by a domain for type zero is defined as follows: the domain of type 0 is the natural domain of type zero ($= ND(t_0)$). If $t = (t_1, t_2, \ldots t_n)$, then $ND(t) =$ the set of all subsets of $ND(t_1) \times ND(t_2) \times \ldots \times ND(t_n)$.

of sets of nonstandard reals, χ. We call the members of χ the *finite sets of nonstandard reals. Some *finite sets contain an infinite number of elements. (For instance, the set of nonstandard natural numbers less than some infinite nonstandard natural number is infinite, yet *finite.) The relation "is the cardinality of" assigns each *finite set a nonstandard natural number as its *nonstandard cardinality*. This allows us to use a *counting measure* for infinite sets which are *finite. A *finite set, F, is called a sample. Relative to such a fixed sample, we can take the *measure of any internal set, A,* as the nonstandard cardinality of its intersection with the sample, F, divided by the nonstandard cardinality of the sample. If A and B are internal sets, we can take the *conditional probability* of B on A as the nonstandard cardinality of the intersection of A, B, and F over the nonstandard cardinality of the intersection of A and F.

Some desirable properties follow from the *finiteness condition on the sample: the measure of the null set is zero; measure is monotonic, if $A \subseteq B$, the measure $A \leqslant$ the measure B; measure is additive. Other desirable properties can be secured by judicious selection of the sample. Bernstein and Wattenberg have shown that there is a sample with the following characteristics: the associated measure is defined for all subsets of the unit interval which is infinitely close to Lebesgue measure for all Lebesgue measurable sets; it assigns each nonempty set a positive (possibly infinitesimal) measure; and it is translation-invariant up to an infinitesimal. (The strategy of the existence proof is to show that the appropriate relation, specifying the desirable properties, is finitely satisfiable.) Parikh and Parnes have carried through the analogous investigation, putting the constraints directly on the conditional probability function and showing the existence of samples which yield associated conditional probabilities with desirable properties. Loeb has studied nonstandard measures on abstract spaces.[4]

4. For details, see these three papers and the references to related work cited therein: A. Bernstein and F. Wattenberg, "Non-Standard Measure Theory," in W. Luxemburg, ed., *Applications of Model Theory to Algebra, Analysis, and Probability* (New York: Holt, Reinhart and

INFINITESIMAL PROBABILITIES

The Vitali-Hausdorff example of a nonmeasurable set shows that no sigma-additive, translation-invariant, real-valued measure can be defined on all subsets of the interval [0, 1). A wheel of fortune is spun and comes to rest with some point or other at the lowest point. We can give the wheel unit circumference and label its points with the numbers in [0, 1). Assume the equiprobable distribution. More specifically, assume that, for any point set, the probability that the wheel stops with a point in that set as the bottommost one is equal to the probability for any point set gotten from the first by displacing each member of the first through a fixed angle, 0 (translation-invariance under addition modulo 1.) Consider the equivalence relation: $x - y$ is rational. This partitions [0, 1), and thus the points in the circumference of our wheel, into equivalence classes. Consider a choice set, C, containing one member of each of these classes. For each rational in [0, 1) let C_r be the set gotten by adding (modulo 1) r to each member of C (i.e., by translating the point set a rational distance around the circumference). There are a denumerable number of C_rs; they are mutually exclusive; and their union is [0, 1). They are equiprobable by translation invariance modulo 1. If propensities are real-valued, then either $\Sigma P_r(C_r) = 0$ or $\Sigma P_r(C_r) = \infty$. If propensities are, furthermore, sigma-additive, then $0 = 1$ or $\infty = 1$.

These difficulties can be overcome if the requirement of sigma additivity is relaxed to that of finite additivity. Banach has shown (as a corollory to the Hahn-Banach theorem) that Lebesgue measure can be extended to a finitely additive, translation-invariant measure defined in all subsets of [0, 1) (indeed, defined on all subsets of the reals). The measure so defined is not, however, regular (strictly coherent). There are sets other than the empty set

Winston, 1969), pp. 171–85; R. Parikh and R. Parnes, "Conditional Probabilities and Uniform Sets," in P. Loeb, ed., *Victoria Symposium on Non-Standard Analysis, 1972* (Heidelberg: Springer, 1974), pp. 180–94; P. Loeb, "A Non-Standard Representation of Borel Measures and σ-Finite Measures," in *Victoria Symposium on Non-Standard Analysis, 1972*, pp. 144–52.

which have Lebesgue measure zero. Thus, on this approach, the probability in our example of the pointer stopping on a rational would be zero, although this might happen. Then the conditional probability (conceived of in the Kolmogoroff way) of stopping on a rational in [0, 1/2) given that it stops on a rational would be undefined. But, as De Finetti and Savage have emphasized, intuitively it should be defined.

The problem is more general than has so far been indicated, however. Lebesgue measure aside, there is no finitely additive, translation-invariant, real-valued measure defined on all subsets of [0, 1) that is *regular*. For, considering the Vitali-Hausdorff example again, the C_rs are equiprobable by translation invariance.[5] If they have a non-zero, real-valued probability, then by the Archimedean property of the reals there is an integer, n, such that n times their probability is greater than 1. Thus finite additivity leads to a contradiction. So the C_rs have zero probability, and the measure is not regular.

If the measure has values in a non-Archimedean ordered field, as in nonstandard analysis, then the paradox is avoided. And, as Bernstein and Wattenberg have shown, there is a finitely additive, almost translation invariant, regular measure defined on all subsets of [0, 1). Nonempty sets of Lebesgue measure zero, as well as the C_rs, then receive infinitesimal measure. And we can say that the probability of our pointer hitting a rational in [0, 1/2), given that it hits a rational, is the ratio of the two appropriate infinitesimals and equals 1/2.

5. Notice that translation invariance implies translation invariance modulo 1.

Selected Bibliography

CHAPTER IA. PROPENSITIES AND STATISTICAL LAWS

Ayer, A. J. "What Is a Law of Nature?" *Revue internationale de philosophie*, vol. 10, no. 2 (1956): 144–65. Reprinted in Ayer, *The Concept of a Person* (New York: St. Martin's, 1968) and in T. Beauchamp, ed., *Philosophical Problems of Causation* (Encino, Cal.: Dickenson, 1974).

Broad, C. D. *Induction, Probability and Causation*. Dordrecht: Reidel, 1968.

Coffa, A. *Randomness and Knowledge*. In Schaffner & Cohen, eds., PSA 1972. Dordrecht: Reidel, 1974 (pp. 103–15).

De Finetti, B. "Foresight, Its Logical Laws, Its Subjective Sources." In H. Kyberg and H. Smokler, eds., *Studies in Subjective Probability*. New York: Wiley, 1964.

———. *Theory of Probability* (2 vols.). New York: Wiley, 1975.

———. *Probability, Induction and Statistics*. New York: Wiley, 1974.

Giere, R. "Objective Single-Case Probabilities and the Foundations of Statistics." In P. Suppes et al., eds., *Logic Methodology and Philosophy of Science IV*. Amsterdam: North Holland, 1973 (pp. 468–83).

Good, I. J. *Probability and the Weighing of Evidence*. New York: Hafner, 1950.

———. *The Estimation of Probabilities*. Cambridge, Mass.: M.I.T. Press, 1965.

Goodman, N. *Fact, Fiction and Forecast*. 2d ed. New York: Bobbs-Merrill, 1965.

Hacking, I. *Logic of Statistical Inference*. Cambridge: Cambridge University Press, 1965.

Hempel, C. G. *Aspects of Scientific Explanation and Other Essays in the Philosophy of Science*. New York: Free Press, 1965.

Jaynes, E. T. *Probability Theory in Science and Engineering*. Colloquium Lectures in Pure and Applied Sci-

ence, no. 4. Field Research Laboratory, Socony Mobil
Oil, Dallas, 1958 (Lecture 5, "The A_p Distribution," pp.
152–87).

Jeffrey, R. The Logic of Decision. New York: Macmillan,
1965.

Keynes, J. M. A Treatise on Probability. London: Macmillan, 1952.

Kyberg, H. "Propensities and Probabilities." British Journal for Philosophy of Science 25 (1974):358–75.

Lewis, D. "A Subjectivist's Guide to Objective Chance." In
R. Jeffrey, ed. Studies in Inductive Logic and Probabil-
ity, vol. 2. Berkeley and Los Angeles: University of
California Press, 1979.

Mellor, H. The Matter of Chance. Cambridge: Cambridge
University Press, 1971.

Mill, J. S. A System of Logic. 8th ed. New York: Harper,
1874.

Pearson, K. The Grammar of Science. London, 1892; New
York: Meridian, 1957.

Popper, K. "The Propensity Interpretation of the Calculus
of Probability and the Quantum Theory." In S. Körner,
ed., Observation and Interpretation in the Philosophy
of Physics. London: Butterworth, 1957.

———. "The Propensity Interpretation of Probability."
British Journal for Philosophy of Science 10
(1959):25–42.

Railton, P. "A Deductive-Nomological Model of Probabilistic Explanation." Philosophy of Science 45
(1978):206–26.

Reichenbach, H. Theory of Probability. Berkeley and Los
Angeles: University of California Press, 1949.

Salmon, W. Statistical Explanation and Statistical Relevance (contributions by W. Salmon, R. Jeffrey, and
J. Greeno). Pittsburgh: University of Pittsburgh Press,
1971.

Savage, L. J. Foundations of Statistics. New York: Wiley,
1954.

Skyrms, B. "Falsifiability in the Logic of Experimental
Tests." Methodos 14 (1962):1–13.

———. "Nomological Necessity and the Paradoxes of

Confirmation." *Philosophy of Science* 33 (1966):230–49.

———. "Physical Laws and the Nature of Philosophical Reduction." *Minnesota Studies in the Philosophy of Science* 7 (ed. Maxwell & Anderson). Minneapolis: University of Minnesota Press, 1975 (pp. 496–529).

———. "Resiliency, Propensity and Causal Necessity." *Journal of Philosophy* (November, 1977): 704–13.

Suppes, P. *A Probabilistic Theory of Causality.* Amsterdam: North Holland, 1970.

van Fraassen, B. "Relative Frequencies." *Synthese* 34: 133–66.

Venn, J. *The Logic of Chance.* 4th ed. New York: Chelsea, 1962.

von Mises, L. *Probability, Statistics and Truth.* London: Allan and Unwin, 1957.

CHAPTER IB. UNIVERSAL LAWS AS LIMITING CASES OF
STATISTICAL LAWS

Ayer, A. J. "What Is a Law of Nature?" *Revue internationale de philosophie,* vol. 10, no. 2 (1956): 144–65. Reprinted in Ayer, *The Concept of a Person* (New York: St. Martin's, 1968) and in T. Beauchamp, ed., *Philosophical Problems of Causation* (Encino, Cal.: Dickenson, 1974).

Bohm, D. *Causality and Chance in Modern Physics.* London: Routledge & Kegan Paul, 1957.

Carnap, R. *Logical Foundations of Probability.* 2d ed. Chicago: University of Chicago Press, 1962.

Goodman, N. *Fact, Fiction and Forecast.* 2d ed. New York: Bobbs-Merrill, 1965.

Hempel, C. G. *Aspects of Scientific Explanation and Other Essays in the Philosophy of Science.* New York: Free Press, 1965.

———. *Philosophy of Science.* New York: Prentice-Hall, 1966.

Hintikka, J. "A Two-Dimensional Continuum of Inductive Methods." In J. Hintikka and P. Suppes, eds., *Aspects of Inductive Logic.* Amsterdam: North Holland, 1966 (pp. 113–32).

Nagel, E. *The Structure of Science.* New York: Harcourt Brace, 1961.

Quine, W. V. O. "Natural Kinds." In Quine, *Ontological Relativity and Other Essays.* New York: Columbia University Press, 1969.

Ramsey, F. P. *The Foundations of Mathematics and Other Logical Essays.* London: Routledge & Kegan Paul, 1931.

Scheffler, I. *The Anatomy of Inquiry.* Indianapolis: Bobbs-Merrill, 1963.

Skyrms, B. "Physical Laws and the Nature of Philosophical Reduction." In *Minnesota Studies in the Philosophy of Science* 7 (ed. Maxwell and Anderson). Minneapolis: University of Minnesota Press, 1975 (pp. 496–529).

———. "Nomological Necessity and the Paradoxes of Confirmation." *Philosophy of Science* 33 (1966): 230–49.

Smokler, H. "The Equivalence Condition." *American Philosophical Quarterly* 4(1967):300–07.

Teller, P. "Conditionalization and Observation." *Synthese* (1973):218–58.

CHAPTER IC. GENERALIZATIONS

Bernstein, A., and Wattenberg, F. "Non-Standard Measure Theory." In W. A. J. Luxemburg, ed., *Applications of Model Theory to Algebra, Analysis and Probability.* New York: Holt, Rinehart & Winston, 1969 (pp. 171–85).

De Finetti, B. *Probability, Induction and Statistics.* New York: Wiley, pp. 67–127.

———. *Theory of Probability I.* New York: Wiley, 1965 (pp. 116–33, 173–78).

Robinson, A. *Introduction to Model Theory and to the Metamathematics of Algebra.* Amsterdam: North Holland, 1965.

———. *Non-Standard Analysis.* Amsterdam: North Holland, 1970.

CHAPTER IIA. CONDITIONALS

Adams, E. "On the Logic of Conditionals." *Inquiry* 8 (1965):166–97.

———. "Probability and the Logic of Conditionals." In Hintikka and Suppes, eds., *Aspects of Inductive Logic*. Amsterdam: North Holland, 1966 (pp. 265–316).

———. *The Logic of Conditionals*. Dordrecht: Reidel, 1975.

———. "Prior Probabilities and Counterfactual Conditionals." In Hooker & Harper, eds., *Proceedings of International Congress on the Foundations of Statistics*. Dordrecht: Reidel, 1975.

Cooper, W. "The Propositional Logic of Ordinary Discourse." *Inquiry* 11 (1968):295–320.

———. *Foundations of Logico-Linguistics*. Dordrecht: Reidel, 1978 (especially ch. 8).

Ellis, B. "Epistemic Foundations of Logic." *Journal of Philosophical Logic* 5 (1976):187–204.

———. "A Unified Theory of Conditionals." La Trobe, December 13, 1976 (mimeographed).

Goodman, N. *Fact, Fiction and Forecast*. 2d ed. Indianapolis: Bobbs-Merrill, 1965.

Grice, H. P. "Logic and Conversation." In Cole and Morgan, eds. *Syntax and Semantics*, vol. 3. New York: Academic Press, 1975.

———. "Logic and Conversation." *The William James Lectures*. Berkeley (manuscript).

———. "Utters' Meaning and Intentions." *Philosophical Review* 78 (1969):147–77.

Lewis, D. "Probabilities of Conditionals and Conditional Probabilities." *Philosophical Review* 85 (1976):297–315.

———. *Counterfactuals*. Cambridge, Mass.: Harvard University Press, 1974.

Skyrms, B. "Contraposition of the Conditional." *Philosophical Studies* 24 (1974):12–14.

Stalnaker, R. "A Theory of Conditionals." In Rescher, ed., *Studies in Logical Theory*. Oxford: Blackwell, 1968.

———. "Probability and Conditionals." *Philosophy of Science* 37 (1970):68–80.

CHAPTER IIB. CAUSE AND EFFECT

§ *IIB1. Causal Relations between Physical* Properties

Blalock, H. M., ed. *Causal Models in the Social Sciences.*
    Chicago: Aldine, 1971.
————. *Causal Inference in Experimental Research.*
    Chapel Hill: University of North Carolina Press, 1964.
Cartwright, N. "Causal Laws and Effective Strategies."
    Stanford, 1978 (mimeographed).
Edgeworth, F. Y. "Correlated Averages." *Philosophical
    Magazine* 34 (1892):191–204.
————. "On the Application of the Calculus of Prob-
    abilities to Statistics." *International Statistical Insti-
    tute Bulletin* (1910):505–36.
Heise, D. *Causal Analysis.* New York: Wiley, 1975.
Jeffrey, R. *The Logic of Decision.* New York: Macmillan,
    1965.
Mill, J. S. *A System of Logic.* 8th ed. New York: Harper,
    1874.
Pearson, K. "Mathematical Contributions to the Theory of
    Evolution." *Proceedings of the Royal Society of Lon-
    don* 60 (1897):489–503.
Salmon, W. *Statistical Explanation and Statistical Rele-
    vance.* Pittsburgh: Pittsburgh University Press, 1971.
Simon, H. *Models of Man.* New York: Wiley, 1957.
Suppes, P. *A Probabilistic Theory of Causality.* Amster-
    dam: North Holland, 1970.
Yule, G. U. "The Applications of the Method of Correla-
    tion to Social and Economic Statistics." *International
    Statistical Institute Bulletin* (1910):537–51.

§ *IIB2. Causal Chains of Physical* Events

INVARIANCE; OPEN AND CLOSED SYSTEMS

Havas, P. "Causality Requirements in the Theory of Rela-
    tivity." In *Boston Studies in the Philosophy of Science*
    5 (ed. R. Cohen and M. Wartofsky). Dordrecht: Reidel,
    1969 (pp. 151–78).

———. "Causality and Relativistic Dynamics." In *Causality and Physical Theories*. American Institute of Physics Conference Proceedings, no. 16 (ed. Rolnick), pp. 23–24.

Wigner, E. "The Role of Invariance Principles in Natural Philosophy." In Moore and Scriven, eds., *Symmetries and Reflections: Scientific Essays of Eugene P. Wigner*. Bloomington: Indiana University Press, 1967.

CAUSAL CHAINS AND THE GEOMETRY OF SPACE-TIME

Ehlers, J., Pirani, F. A. E., and Schild, A. "The Geometry of Free Fall and Light Propagation." In L. O'Raifeartaigh, ed., *General Relativity: Essays in Honor of J. L. Synge*. London: Oxford University Press, 1972 (pp. 63–84).

Grünbaum, A. *Philosophical Problems of Space and Time*. 2d ed. Boston: Reidel, 1974.

Hawking, S., and Ellis, G. *The Large Scale Structure of Space-Time*. London: Cambridge University Press, 1973 (especially ch. 6).

Latzer, R. W. "Nondirected Light Signals and the Structure of Time." *Synthese* 24:236–80.

Malament, D. "Causal Theories of Time and the Conventionality of Simultaneity." *Nous*, vol. 11, no. 3 (1977):293–99.

Misner, C., Thorne, K., and Wheeler, J. A. *Gravitation*. San Francisco: Freeman, 1973.

Ohanian, H. *Gravitation and Space-Time*. New York: Norton, 1976 (especially chs. 2 & 5).

Zeeman, E. C. "Causality Implies the Lorentz Group." *Journal of Mathematical Physics* 5 (1964):490–93.

LOCALITY IN RELATIVITY THEORY

Van Dam, H., and Wigner, E. "Instantaneous and Asymptotic Conservation Laws for Classical Relativistic Mechanics of Interacting Point Particles." *Physical Review*, vol. 142, no. 4 (February 1966):838–43.

See also the relevant sections in Ohanian and in Misner, Thorne, and Wheeler (cited in the immediately preceding section of the bibliography).

TACHYONS

Earman, J. "Implications of Causal Propagation Outside
   the Null Cone." *Australasian Journal of Philosophy,*
   vol. 50, no. 3 (1972):222–37.

ASYMMETRY

Davies. P. C. W. *The Physics of Time Asymmetry.* Berke-
   ley and Los Angeles: University of California Press,
   1977.
Earman, J. "Causality, a Matter of Life and Death." *Journal
   of Philosophy,* vol. 63, no. 1 (1976):5–25.
Reichenbach, H. *The Direction of Time.* Berkeley and Los
   Angeles: University of California Press, 1971.
Terletskii, Y. *Paradoxes in the Theory of Relativity.* New
   York: Plenum Press, 1968.
Wheeler, J. A., and Feynman, R. "Interaction with the Ab-
   sorber as the Mechanism of Radiation." *Reviews of
   Modern Physics* 17 (1945):157–81.

LOCALITY IN QUANTUM THEORY

Belinfante, F. J. *A Survey of Hidden Variables Theories.*
   New York: Pergamon, 1973.
Bell, J. S. "On the Einstein-Podolsky-Rosen Paradox."
   Physics (1965):195–200.
————. "On the Problem of Hidden Variables in Quantum
   Mechanics." *Reviews of Modern Physics* 38
   (1966):447–75.
————. "Introduction to the Hidden Variable Question."
   In B. d'Espagnat, ed., *Foundations of Quantum
   Mechanics.* New York: Academic Press, 1971.
Clauser, J. F., and Horne, M. A. "Experimental Conse-
   quences of Objective Local Theories." *Physical Re-
   view D,* vol. 10, no. 2 (1974):526–32.
Clauser, J. F., Horne, M. A., Shimony, A., and Holt, R. A.
   Physical Review Letters 23 (1969):880.
Eberhard, P. "Bell's Theorem without Hidden Variables."
   Il Nuovo Cimento, vol. 38B, no. 1 (1977):75–79.
d'Espagnat, B. *Conceptual Foundations of Quantum
   Mechanics.* 2d. ed. Reading, Mass.: Benjamin, 1976.
   Part 3, "Quantum Non-Separability," is a very clear
   and careful discussion of these problems.

Shimony, A. "The Status of Hidden-Variable Theories."
In P. Suppes et al., eds., *Logic, Methodology, and Philosophy of Science IV*. Amsterdam: North Holland,
1973.

Stapp, H. P. "S-Matrix Interpretation of Quantum
Theory." *Physical Review D*, vol. 3, no. 6
(1971):1303–20.

———. "Bell's Theorem and World Process." *Il Nuovo
Cimento*, vol. 29B, no. 2 (1975):270–76.

Wigner, E. "On Hidden Variables and Quantum Mechanical Probabilities." *American Journal of Physics* 38
(1970):1005–09.

CHAPTER IIC. THE ROLE OF CAUSAL FACTORS IN RATIONAL
DECISION

Cartwright, N. "Causal Laws and Effective Strategies."
Stanford, 1978 (mimeographed).

Gibbard, A., and Harper, W. "Counterfactuals and Two
Kinds of Expected Utility." Discussion Paper 194,
Center for Mathematical Studies in Economics and
Management Science. Northwestern University
(Evanston, Illinois).

Jeffrey, R. *The Logic of Decision*. New York: McGraw-Hill,
1965.

———. "Savage's Omelet." In *PSA 1976* 2:361–71.

Nozick, R. "Newcomb's Paradox and Two Principles of
Choice." In Rescher et al., eds., *Essays in Honor of Carl
G. Hempel*. Dordrecht: Reidel, 1969.

Savage, L. J. *The Foundations of Statistics*. New York:
Dover, 1972 (originally published 1954).

CHAPTER IID. SCIENTIFIC EXPLANATION

Ellis, B. "Explanation and the Logic of Support." *Australasian Journal of Philosophy*, vol. 148, no. 2 (August 1970):177–89.

Jeffrey, R. "Statistical Explanation vs. Statistical Inference." In Rescher, ed., *Essays in Honor of Carl G.
Hempel*. Dordrecht: Reidel, 1969 (pp. 104–13). Reprinted in W. Salmon, *Statistical Explanation and*

Statistical Relevance (Pittsburgh: University of
    Pittsburgh Press, 1971), pp. 19–28.

Hempel, C. G. "Aspects of Scientific Explanation." New
    York: Free Press, 1965.

Ninniluoto, I. "Inductive Explanation, Propensity and Ac-
    tion." In Manninen and Tuomela, eds., *Essays in Ex-
    planation and Understanding.* Dordrecht: Reidel,
    1976 (pp. 335–68).

Railton, P. "A Deductive-Nomological Model of Prob-
    abilistic Explanation." *Philosophy of Science* 45
    (1978):206–26.

Rescher, N., and Skyrms, B. "A Methodological Problem
    in the Evaluation of Explanations." *Nous* (May
    1968):121–29.

Skyrms, B. "Falsifiability in the Logic of Experimental
    Tests." *Methodos* 16 (1962):3–13.

Salmon, W. "Statistical Explanation." In R. Colodny, ed.,
    Nature and Function of Scientific Theories.
    Pittsburgh: University of Pittsburgh Press, 1970 (pp.
    173–231). Reprinted in Salmon, W. *Statistical Expla-
    nation and Statistical Relevance* (Pittsburgh: Univer-
    sity of Pittsburgh Press, 1971), with further comments.

Scriven, M. "Explanation and Prediction in Evolutionary
    Theory." *Science* 130 (1959).

————. "Explanations, Predictions and Laws." In *Min-
    nesota Studies in the Philosophy of Science* 3 (ed.
    Feigl and Maxwell). Minneapolis: University of Min-
    nesota Press, 1962 (pp. 170–230).

CHAPTER IIE. KNOWLEDGE

Armstrong, D. *Belief, Truth and Knowledge* (London:
    Cambridge University Press, 1973).

Gettier, E. "Is Justified True Belief Knowledge?" Analysis
    23 (1963). Reprinted in M. Roth and L. Gallis, eds.,
    Knowing: Essays in the Analysis of Knowledge (New
    York: Random House, 1970).

Goldman, A. "A Causal Theory of Knowing." *Journal of
    Philosophy* 64 (1967):357–72.

Harman, G. *Thought.* Princeton: Princeton University
    Press, 1973.

Lehrer, K. *Knowledge.* Oxford: Clarendon Press, 1974.
Lehrer, K., and Paxson, T. "Knowledge: Undefeated Jus-
  tified True Belief." *Journal of Philosophy* 64
  (1969):225–37.
Ramsey, F. P. *The Foundations of Mathematics and Other
  Logical Essays.* London: Routledge & Kegan Paul,
  1931.
Russell, B. *Human Knowledge, Its Scope and Limits.* New
  York: Simon & Schuster, 1948.
Skyrms, B. "The Explication of 'X Knows that p.'" *Journal
  of Philosophy* 64 (1967):373–89. Reprinted in M. Roth
  and L. Gallis, eds., *Knowing: Essays in the Analysis of
  Knowledge* (New York: Random House, 1970).

CHAPTER IIF. RESILIENCY AND RULES OF ACCEPTANCE

Harman, G. *Thought.* Princeton: Princeton University
  Press, 1973.
Hilpinen, R. *Rules of Acceptance and Inductive Logic.*
  Amsterdam: North Holland, 1968.
Kyberg, H. "Probability, Rationality and a Rule of De-
  tachment." In Bar-Hillel, ed., *Logic, Methodology and
  Philosophy of Science.* Amsterdam: North Holland,
  1965.
———. "Conjunctivitis." In M. Swain, ed., *Induction, Ac-
  ceptance and Rational Belief.* Dordrecht: Reidel, 1970.
Levi, I. *Gambling with Truth.* New York: Knopf, 1967.
———. "Acceptance Revisited." In Bogdan, ed., *Local In-
  duction.* Dordrecht: Reidel, 1976.

APPENDIX 2. SECOND-ORDER PROBABILITIES AND FALLIBLE
  LEARNING

Good, I. J. *The Estimation of Probabilities, an Essay on
  Modern Bayesian Methods.* Research Monograph no.
  30. Cambridge, Mass.: M.I.T. Press, 1965.
Jamison, D. "Bayesian Information Usage." In J. Hintikka
  and P. Suppes, eds., *Information and Inference.* Dordrecht: Reidel, 1970.
Jaynes, E. T. *Probability Theory in Science and Engineering.* Colloquim Lectures in Pure and Applied Science,

no. 4. Field Research Laboratory, Socony Mobil Oil, Dallas, 1958 (Lecture 5, "The A$_p$ Distribution," pp. 152–87).

Jeffrey, R. "Preference among Preferences." *Journal of Philosophy,* vol. 71, no. 13 (July 1974):377–91.

Teller, P. "Conditionalization and Observation." *Synthese* (1973):218–58.

APPENDIX 3. ITERATED PROBABILITY CONDITIONALS AND LEWIS'S TRIVIALITY PROOF

Adams, E. *The Logic of Conditionals: An Application of Probability to Deductive Logic.* Dordrecht: Reidel, 1975.

Jeffrey, R. *The Logic of Decision.* New York: Macmillan, 1965.

Lewis, D. "Probabilities of Conditionals and Conditional Probabilities." *Philosophical Review,* vol. 85, no. 3 (1976):297–315.

Stalnaker, R. "A Theory of Conditionals." In Rescher, ed., *Studies in Logical Theory.* Oxford: Blackwell, 1968.

———. "Probabilities and Conditionals." *Philosophy of Science* 37 (1970):68–80.

APPENDIX 4. NONSTANDARD ANALYSIS AND INFINITESIMAL PROBABILITIES

Bell, J. L., and Slomson, A. B. *Models and Ultraproducts.* Amsterdam: North Holland, 1969.

Bernstein, A., and Wattenberg, F. "Non-Standard Measure Theory." In W. A. J. Luxemburg, ed., *Applications of Model Theory of Algebra, Analysis and Probability.* New York: Holt, Rinehart & Winston, 1969 (pp. 171–85).

Boolos, G., and Jeffrey, R. *Computability and Logic.* London: Cambridge University Press, 1974 (ch. 17).

Enderton, H. *A Mathematical Introduction to Logic.* New York: Academic Press, 1972 (section 2.8, "Nonstandard Analysis").

Henkin, L. "The Completeness of the First-Order

Functional Calculus." *Journal of Symbolic Logic* 14
(1949):159–66.

———. "Completeness in the Theory of Types." *Journal of
Symbolic Logic* 15 (1960):81–91.

Henson, C. "On Nonstandard Representation of Measures." *Transactions of the American Mathematical
Society* 172 (October 1972):437–46.

Loeb, P. "A Nonstandard Representation of Borel Mea-
sures and σ-Finite Measures." *Victoria Symposium on
Nonstandard Analysis, 1972* (ed. P. Loeb et al.).
Heidelberg: Springer, 1974 (pp. 144–52).

Parikh, R., and Parnes, R. "Conditional Probabilities and
Uniform Sets." *Victoria Symposium on Nonstandard
Analysis, 1972* (ed. Loeb et al.). Heidelberg: Springer,
1974 (pp. 180–94).

Robinson, A. *Non-Standard Analysis*. Amsterdam: North
Holland, 1966.

Royden, H. *Real Analysis*. New York: Macmillan, 1968.

Index